Contemporary

SOFTBALL

Loren Walsh

 Contemporary Books, Inc.
Chicago

Library of Congress Cataloging in Publication Data

Walsh, Loren.
    Contemporary softball.

    Includes index.
    1. Softball.   I. Title.
GV881.W33   1978   796.357'8   77-91302
ISBN 0-8092-7555-4
ISBN 0-8092-7628-3 pbk.

Illustrated by Anghelo

All photography by "Chick" Walsh unless indicated otherwise.

Copyright © 1978 by Loren Walsh
All rights reserved
Published by Contemporary Books, Inc.
180 North Michigan Avenue, Chicago, Illinois 60601
Manufactured in the United States of America
Library of Congress Catalog Card Number: 77-91302
International Standard Book Number: 0-8092-7555-4 (cloth)
                                     0-8092-7628-3 (paper)

Published simultaneously in Canada by
Beaverbooks
953 Dillingham Road
Pickering, Ontario L1W 1Z7
Canada

1
History and introduction

According to historians, the game of softball originated in Chicago, Illinois. On Thanksgiving Day, 1887, a group of young men at the Farragut Boat Club were awaiting the telegraph returns on the results of the Yale-Harvard football game.

While passing the time, one of the young men threw an old boxing glove at a friend. He in turn hit it with a broomstick. A young man named George Hancock then grabbed the glove, tied it into a sphere, and shouted, "Let's play ball!" Teams were chosen, and the first softball game began.

After the game, Hancock made a crude ball somewhat larger than a regular baseball. He compiled a list of rules for playing the game in an area much smaller than a baseball field. In fact, it could be played and was played in a gymnasium. The new game was called Indoor Baseball.

Several teams were made up during the winter of 1887, and the game became very popular in Chicago. In a few short years the game spread to other parts of the country. The first set of standard rules was published by Hancock in 1889 and sold in many parts of the United States.

Many different rules were used by many different teams as the game continued its rapid growth. At one point in the history of the game, it was estimated that at least a dozen different sizes of balls were in use. Bats varied considerably in length, weight, and design.

Eventually a committee, the Amateur Softball Association (ASA), met in 1933 to establish a standard set of rules. Later on, the committee became known as the International Joint Rules Committee on Softball (IJRC). Today softball is played worldwide with one standard set of rules.

More than 26 million adults and children play softball in the United States. Softball is presently the nation's most popular and largest team sport. Even though a standard set of rules has been established, there are still three sizes of balls in

Figure 1.1 Today more than 26 million adults and children play softball in the United States.

use: 12-inch, 14-inch, and 16-inch. At present the 12-inch version is by far the most common. In the early years of the game the 12-inch fast pitch was the most popular. In recent years, however, the 12-inch slow pitch has taken over as the leading U.S. team participation sport.

National tournament

The first fast-pitch national tournament for both men and women was held in 1933 in Chicago. From 1933 through 1939 the national tournament remained in Chicago. It was played in Detroit from 1940 through 1943. Cleveland, Ohio, became host city for the games from 1944 through 1947. In 1948, Portland, Oregon, was selected as the site for the tournament.

In 1949, for the first time, the men's and women's tournaments were held at different locations. Since then—except for 1951, when both men's and women's tournaments were held in Detroit—the tournaments have been staged in different cities.

During the first ten years of the nationals no team won the men's championship two years in a row. Then in 1943 and 1944 Hammer Field of Fresno, California, was crowned national champion for both years. In 1945 the Zollner Piston team from Fort Wayne, Indiana, took the national men's title and went on in 1946 and 1947 to become the first and only team to win the title three years in a row.

After holding the title for three straight years, the Piston team elected not to enter the national tournament again. Most softball experts believe that the Zollner Pistons could have won the national title at least five more times if they had continued to compete.

The Zollner organization was one of several companies that helped establish the great National Fastball League. This league, one of the finest fast-pitch leagues ever organized, operated from 1946 until 1950, when it was temporarily disbanded because of the Korean War. It disbanded permanently in 1954. The final game for the league play-off championship was played in Aurora, Illinois, between Briggs Beautyware, of Detroit and the Aurora Sealmasters on September 14, 1954. Detroit won the final game 3-2, in eight innings. Detroit's John Spring, later elected to the ASA Hall of Fame, defeated Aurora's Loren "Chick" Walsh, author of *Inside Softball* and *Contemporary Softball*.

The Clearwater (Florida) Bombers won the National Championship at Austin, Texas, in 1950. Three teams—the Clearwater Bombers, the Raybestos Cardinals of Stratford, Connecticut, and the Aurora Sealmasters—dominated the Nationals from 1950 to 1973.

The Women's Fast-Pitch National Tournament was also dominated by three teams. The Jax Maids (New Orleans, Louisiana), the Lionettes (Orange, California), and the Raybestos Brakettes (Stratford, Connecticut) combined to win 25 titles from 1942 through 1973.

First women's world tournament

Melbourne, Australia, was the site of the first worldwide Women's Fast-Pitch championship in 1965. Although highly favored, the U.S. team was defeated by the Australians 1-0 in the final game. In 1970 the second women's world tournament was held in Japan. A record crowd of more than 30,000 witnessed the final game between the U.S. and Japan, which the U.S. team once more was highly favored to win. But the U.S. went down to defeat, 1-0, this time at the hands of the Japanese women, who ended with a 9-1 record.

In 1974, 15 teams competed for the Women's World Championship at Stratford, Connecticut. For the first time the participating teams were divided into two divisions. A round robin, plus a play-off series, decided the winner. With a record of 9 wins and no defeats, the U.S. team became world champion for the first time.

First men's world tournament

Represented by the Aurora Sealmasters, the U.S. was the winner of the first Men's Fast-Pitch World Championship Tournament in 1966 at Mexico City, Mexico (Figure 1.2). The Sealmasters completely dominated the play and came in first with a record of 10 wins and no losses. The U.S., once again represented by the Sealmasters, became world champions in 1968 at Oklahoma City, Oklahoma, with a 10-1 record.

Ten teams competed in the 1972 world championship at Manila, Philippines. Canada emerged as the winner, with the U.S., represented by Welty Way of Cedar Rapids, Iowa, finishing second.

Figure 1.2 Aurora Sealmasters represented the U.S.A. in the first Men's Fast-Pitch World Championship held in Mexico City in 1966. The U.S.A. won with a record of 10 victories and no defeats.

Slow pitch

Slow pitch, particularly 16- and 14-inch, has been played since the beginning of the game. Nevertheless, the tremendous growth of 12-inch slow pitch in the 1950s and 1960s can be attributed to the decline of interest in fast pitch. Many reasons have been offered as to why the popularity of fast pitch declined. The overwhelming dominance of pitching was probably the main factor. Of course, there were other reasons, but the end result was the emergence of a new game, 12-inch slow pitch—by far the most popular team sport in America today. Many tournaments, as well as national championships, are held for both men's and women's teams.

Regulation playing field

An official softball field (Figure 1.3) consists of a clear area that lies between the foul lines and 25 feet outside the foul lines. The field should not have any obstructions within a radius from home plate, as in the following specifications:

225 feet (male and female fast pitch)
250 feet (female slow pitch)
275 feet (male slow pitch)

HOME PLATE AREA.

NOTES:
1. Pitching distance:
   fast pitch   male 46'
                female 40'
   slow pitch   male 46'
                female 46'

2. Outfield fence distance:
   fast pitch   male 225'
                female 225'
   slow pitch   male 275'
                female 250'

3. Outside the foul lines and between home plate and the backstop, there shall be an unobstructed area of not less than 25 feet in width.

6

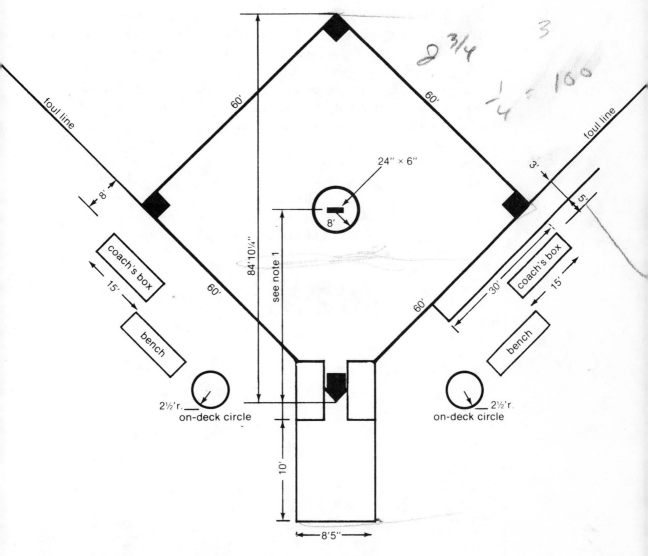

Figure 1.3 Official playing field specifications.

Whenever possible, the field should be enclosed by a fence. An enclosed field avoids the need for many confusing ground rules. However, if the field is not enclosed, ground rules covering obstacles must be established by league officials or an agreement must be made between opposing teams before each game to avoid complications.

When laying out a new field, be sure to place home plate so that the sun will be behind the catcher. Always start the layout of the field from home plate. Once home plate is located, drive a stake at the corner nearest the catcher. Attach a cord to the stake and tie or mark four points at the following distances: 46 feet; 60 feet; 84 feet, 10¼ inches; and 120 feet. Without stretching it, draw the cord taut and walk toward the center of the diamond. With the cord tight and cutting home plate into two equal parts, place the 46-foot marker on the ground and drive a stake at this point. This stake will locate the middle of the front edge of the pitcher's rubber. A distance of 46 feet is correct for all softball diamonds (Figure 1.4) unless the diamond is to be used for

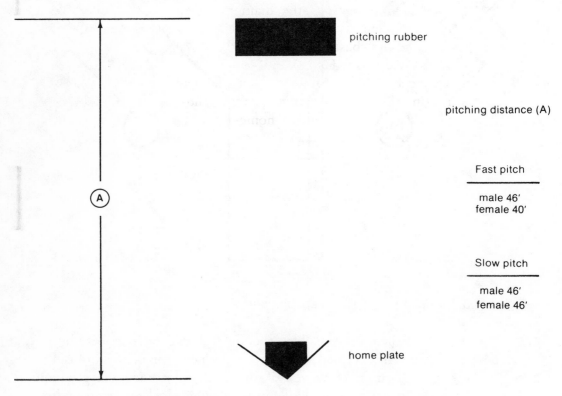

Figure 1.4 Official pitching distances.

Contents

female fast pitch. Women's fast-pitch rules require a pitching distance of 40 feet.

Once the pitching plate has been set, continue in the same line with the cord until you reach the 84-foot, 10¼-inch mark. With the cord taut, drive a stake at this point. This will be the center of second base. Locate the 120-foot marker on the cord and tie it to the second-base stake. Then find the 60-foot marker and walk away from the line at home plate and second base toward the left-field foul line. Once the line becomes taut at the 60-foot marker, drive another stake. Repeat this procedure on the other side of second base toward the right-field foul line. Once again drive a stake at the 60-foot marker. These two stakes will determine the outside corners of first base and third base.

Always recheck the diamond layout in the following manner. Remove the cord from the home-plate stake and tie it to the first-base stake. Then tie the 120-foot marker to the third-base stake. Hold the 60-foot marker and walk toward second base. If the field has been laid out correctly, the 60-foot marker will check out at the second-base stake. It should also check out with the home-plate stake in the opposite direction. It's a good idea to check all distances again with a steel tape measure.

Equipment

In most cases, bats will be furnished by the team organization. Because softball bats come in various lengths, weights, shapes, and materials, the player usually has a good chance of finding a bat that meets his or her needs. The bat used should be an official softball bat clearly marked "Official Softball" by the manufacturer.

An official bat (Figure 1.5) must be round and can be made from wood (one piece), metal, bamboo, plastic, or laminated wood. It must not exceed 38 ounces in weight.

Metal bats must be free of burrs and any rough or sharp

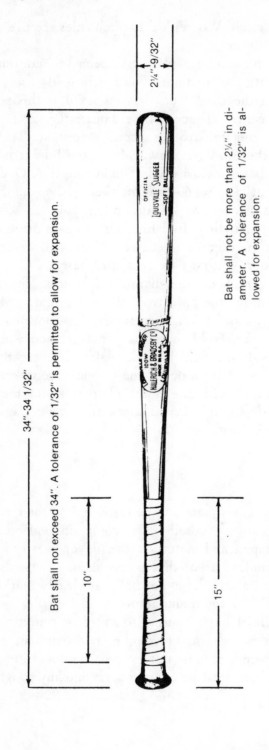

2¼" - 9/32"

Bat shall not be more than 2¼" in diameter. A tolerance of 1/32" is allowed for expansion.

34"-34 1/32"

Bat shall not exceed 34". A tolerance of 1/32" is permitted to allow for expansion.

10"

15"

Safety grip shall be no less than 10" long. It shall not extend more than 15" from small end of bat.

OFFICIAL
LOUISVILLE SLUGGER
SOFT BALL

TEMPER

100W
HILLERICH & BRADSBY CO
LOUISVILLE

Figure 1.5   The official softball bat.

corners. They cannot have wooden handles. Wooden bats must be made either from one piece of hard wood or from a block of laminated wood. Plastic and bamboo bats have no special requirements other than those mentioned for the other types of softball bats.

An official softball bat must not be longer than 34 inches or have a diameter greater than $2\frac{9}{32}$ inches. All bats must have some type of safety grip of cork, tape, or composition material. The safety grip should be at least 10 inches long and should not extend more than 15 inches from the small end of the bat.

The official softball measures between $11\frac{7}{8}$ and $12\frac{1}{8}$ inches in circumference, weighs between $6\frac{1}{2}$ and 7 ounces, and has a center made of fibre kapok or of a cork-rubber mixture. The ball is covered in chrome-tanned horsehide or cowhide sewed in a seamless stitch with waxed thread. Cement applied to the underside of the covering holds it to the ball.

Personal Equipment

Most teams require the player to furnish his own shoes and glove. Metal shoe spikes may be used if the spikes are no higher than three-fourths of an inch. Rounded metal spikes, such as track or golf spikes, are not allowed.

A ball player's glove or mitt (Figure 1.6) is the most important tool of his trade. A conscientious player not only keeps the glove always with him on the field, he also keeps it free from dirt and in fine condition. Official rules permit any member of a team to wear a glove, but only the catcher and the first baseman are allowed to wear a mitt.

Pitchers are required to wear a glove of one color other than white or gray. All other players may wear multicolored gloves providing that the gloves do not have white or gray circles that give the appearance of a ball.

The rules require a catcher to wear a mask in fast pitch

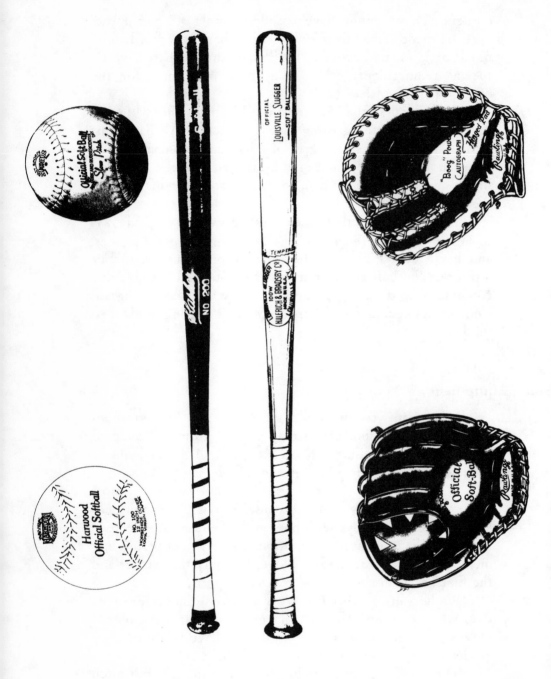

Figure 1.6   Equipment used for slow pitch and fast pitch.

and recommend one for slow pitch. Other catching equipment includes a chest protector and shin guards. In most cases the team sponsor will furnish the catcher's equipment as well as the batting helmets.

Uniforms of all players must be identical in color, trim and style. Undershirts that are exposed to view and worn by more than one team member should be of the same color. Ragged or torn sleeves on uniform shirts or undershirts are not permitted. Caps are part of the official uniform.

Photograph by R. Schreul

2

Infield basics

A softball infielder, in both fast pitch and slow pitch, must be able to get rid of batted ground balls more rapidly than a baseball infielder. Base paths in baseball measure 90 feet, but in softball the distance is only 60 feet. As a result, the softball infielder must have good reactions. He must field and throw the ball much faster than the baseball infielder.

Box score results show that the majority of defensive plays are made in the infield. However, box scores do not show how difficult each particular play can be. Some plays in the infield are very easy and can be made by nearly anyone. But most are difficult bounces, spinning grounders, or well-placed bunts. A good infielder must cleanly field all types of hit or bunted balls and then throw accurately to the proper base for the putout.

Stance (fast pitch and slow pitch)

Many different stances are used by infielders in softball

and baseball. A semi-crouch with hands on knees or a semi-crouch with your throwing hand in your glove (Figure 2.1) are the most common types of stances. Another stance used is the full crouch, with both hands extended toward the ground. Regardless of which stance you choose, your legs should be well spread, with your weight on the ball of the foot. This allows you to move forward, backward, left, or right with little lost motion. A beginner should try several stances to find the one that is the most comfortable.

Figure 2.1   Infielder in the typical
ready position.

Ground balls (fast pitch and slow pitch)

Fielding a ground ball properly is a skill that must be mastered by the infielder. One of the first things to learn is to keep your glove close to the ground. Ground balls are handled more easily when you bring the glove from the ground up, so don't try to put your glove down at the last moment. When an infielder sees a ground ball coming toward him, he should get the glove down immediately. If you remember this very basic instruction, you will be able to keep tricky hops from going under the glove.

Besides getting the glove down quickly, there are two other rules that an infielder should always remember: (1) whenever possible, get in front of the ball (Figure 2.2); and (2) always play the ball; don't let it play you.

No matter how well a field is maintained, it's hard to predict what a grounder will do. That's why it's so impor-

Figure 2.2   Get in front of a ground ball with feet well spread.

tant to get in front of the ball, keeping your glove near the ground (Figure 2.3). If you just reach for a ball, any unusual hop can cause it to bounce over your glove. But if you get in front of it, even a tricky hop will usually hit some part of the body, which will prevent the ball from going into the out-field.

Playing the ball rather than letting it play you takes practice. Playing the ball means that the fielder moves in and

Figure 2.3   Glove should be low and close to the ground, the throwing hand ready to clasp ball.

Figure 2.4   Let ball roll into glove and firmly clasp hand on ball.

toward a grounder rather than letting it come to him. Waiting for the easy bounce makes it easier to field a ground ball, but it usually allows the runner to beat the throw.

A beginning infielder should start out by having someone hit slow-moving balls directly to him or her. As the ball approaches, cup the glove slightly and let the fingertips touch the ground. Let the ball roll into the cupped glove and then quickly and firmly clasp the throwing hand over the ball (Figure 2.4).

After you become accustomed to fielding grounders hit directly at you, practice going to both your left and your right. Remember to keep your glove low, as you did for those balls hit directly to you.

Accurate throws (fast pitch and slow pitch)

Throwing accurately and getting rid of the ball quickly are more important than throwing hard. To throw properly requires good footwork as well as correct arm motion. Proper pivoting and planting of the front foot are key factors in making good throws.

The beginning infielder tends to go through several distinct jerky motions when first learning to field and throw the ground ball. Don't be too concerned about this. Eventually, scooping up the ball, pivoting, planting the front foot, and throwing will become one smooth motion.

Although he must get rid of the ball very quickly, an infielder often makes the mistake of trying to throw the ball before he has it. Never look at the runner. Trying to watch the runner and field the ball usually causes you to hurry the throw. Keep your eye on the ball until it has gone into your glove. Then practice getting a firm grip on the ball before throwing. After much practice and concentration you will be able to get rid of the ball quickly as well as throw accurately.

Learning when not to throw is just as important as

throwing accurately. Trying to throw out a runner with a hard, hurried throw can be costly. If there is a doubt that you can get the runner, hold the throw. A wild throw not only fails to get the runner out, it usually means that he may advance one, two, or even three bases.

Handling pop-ups (fast pitch and slow pitch)

On a simple pop-up, quickly position yourself directly under it rather than trying to reach out for the ball. Keep your eyes glued to the ball as it falls all the way into your glove. Keeping your eyes on it is more important than how you catch it. Some players like to catch the pop-up by forming a basket with their glove and bare hand (Figure 2.5). Others prefer to catch it with both hands held over their heads (Figure 2.6). Either way is acceptable.

After catching a pop fly, be very careful what you do with the ball. Always stay alert after the catch. For example, if you go after a ball that carries you away from your position, a runner may attempt to take an extra base after the catch. A runner may also try to bluff you by acting as if he is about to take off for the next base. He is trying to get you to make a long throw, particularly to the base he has just left. Don't be fooled by such a fake. Hold on to the ball and immediately run back into the infield area, still watching the runner. Keep your eyes on him at all times and throw only if he makes a break for the next base.

Trapped runner (fast pitch and slow pitch)

Sometimes a runner gets too far off the base and finds himself trapped. Once a runner is obviously off the base too far, an infielder has three choices. Number one is to run him down yourself and tag him out. Another choice is to run him down with the help of another infielder. If you are unable to run him down, your third choice is to run him back to the original base he rounded.

Figure 2.5   Some players prefer to catch infield pop-ups by forming a basket with both hands.

Figure 2.6   Most infielders catch pop-ups with glove held above head. Throwing hand is ready to clasp ball.

Figure 2.7   Rundowns should be practiced often. The back up man protects base.

Whenever possible, four defensive men should be used to complete the rundown. Besides the two players handling the ball on the rundown, two others should be backing them up at both bases involved. This is done just in case the runner should get by the two fielders handling the ball.

Practicing rundowns is a good idea (Figure 2.7), whether the players are beginners or experienced ball players. There should be as few throws as possible during the rundown. An infielder must learn to fake throws well in order to fool the runner into stopping his forward progress. The tag is made much easier in this manner.

Infield placement (fast pitch)

There are three set positions for the fast-pitch infield: (1) regular depth (Figure 2.8); (2) bunt or cutoff depth (Figure 2.9); and, (3) double-play depth (Figure 2.10). The

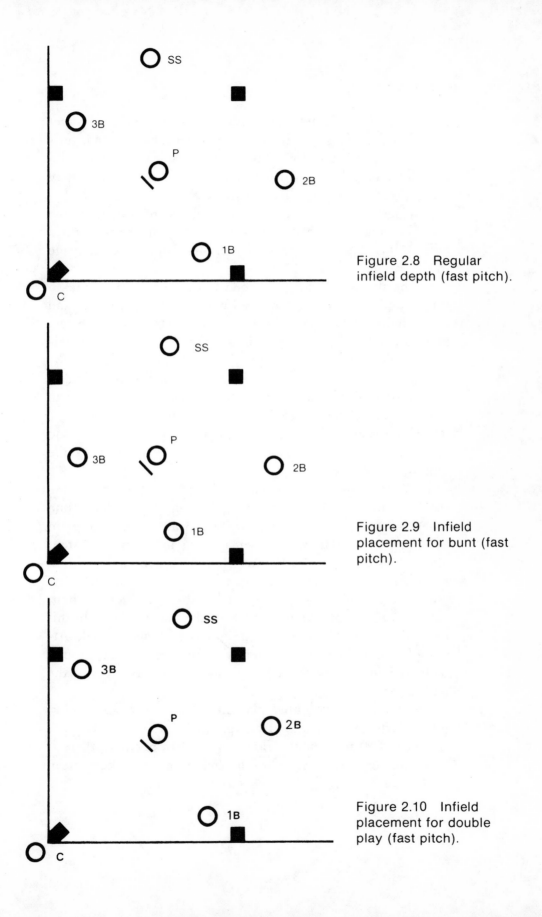

Figure 2.8   Regular infield depth (fast pitch).

Figure 2.9   Infield placement for bunt (fast pitch).

Figure 2.10   Infield placement for double play (fast pitch).

third and first basemen play anywhere from two to ten feet in front of the bag. There are many variations in the player's "regular depth" positions. For example, with two out and a hard-hitting right-handed batter up, the third baseman may play only two or three feet in front of the bag. Yet, with a speedy left-handed batter at bat in the same situation, the third baseman may play as far as ten feet in front of third base. In fast pitch every batter presents a different challenge to the infield.

The shortstop and the second baseman play from one to three steps in front of the grass portion of the outfield and about halfway between the bases. A shortstop or a second baseman will vary their positions from side to side, depending on the hitter. If the hitter is right-handed and a well-known pull-hitter, the second baseman will move several steps closer to second. The shortstop will play deeper than normal and "cheat" a few steps toward third base. This same infield position will be taken by the shortstop and second baseman with a left-handed hitter who often hits to the opposite field.

With a strong left-handed pull-hitter at the plate, the shortstop moves a few steps toward second base. The second baseman plays slightly deeper and a couple of steps closer to first than usual. The third baseman pulls in a couple of steps and moves a step or two toward the pitcher, and the first baseman plays deeper and closer to the bag than usual.

"Double-play" depth is used with a runner on first, runners on first and second, or with the bases loaded. In this case, the infielders are drawn in closer than normal. Although this reduces the infielders' range for fielding ground balls, it is necessary to sacrifice range in order to get to the ball faster.

Completing a double play in softball is no easy task, particularly in the game of fast pitch. Because the base path distance is 60 feet, in contrast to 90 feet in baseball, there is no room for mistakes. First, the fielder must make a clean

pickup, get the ball out of his glove, and make an accurate throw. A second fielder has to make a clean catch and complete another accurate throw. A third fielder must get to the bag and make a clean catch before the second runner hits the base. This entire action must be completed within three to four seconds.

To cut off a run at home or to field a sacrifice bunt requires another type of infield position. Every infielder is drawn in closer than the double-play depth position. The third and first basemen play in very close. Sometimes they will play within ten feet of the hitter on an obvious bunt situation.

Infield placement (slow pitch)

A slow-pitch infield uses the following three patterns: (1) regular depth (Figure 2.11); (2) double-play depth (Figure 2.12); and, (3) tight infield depth (Figure 2.13).

Since bunting is not allowed in the game of slow pitch, "regular depth" is different than it is in fast pitch. Both the first and third basemen play much deeper in slow pitch, and the shortstop and second baseman usually play slightly deeper. The first and third basemen play even with or slightly behind the bag. The second baseman and shortstop play almost at the edge of the grass section of the outfield.

All the infielders are drawn in for the "double-play" depth. At this point the first and third basemen move in about six to eight feet in front of their respective bases. Besides moving in about six to eight feet, the shortstop and second baseman both cheat a little toward second base. As in fast pitch, this placement cuts down on their fielding range, but it is necessary in order to get to the ball in time to make a "twin killing." In slow pitch, the pitcher becomes very important to the infield strategy. Once the pitcher releases the ball, he quickly moves back several steps, situating himself in a better position to field the ball.

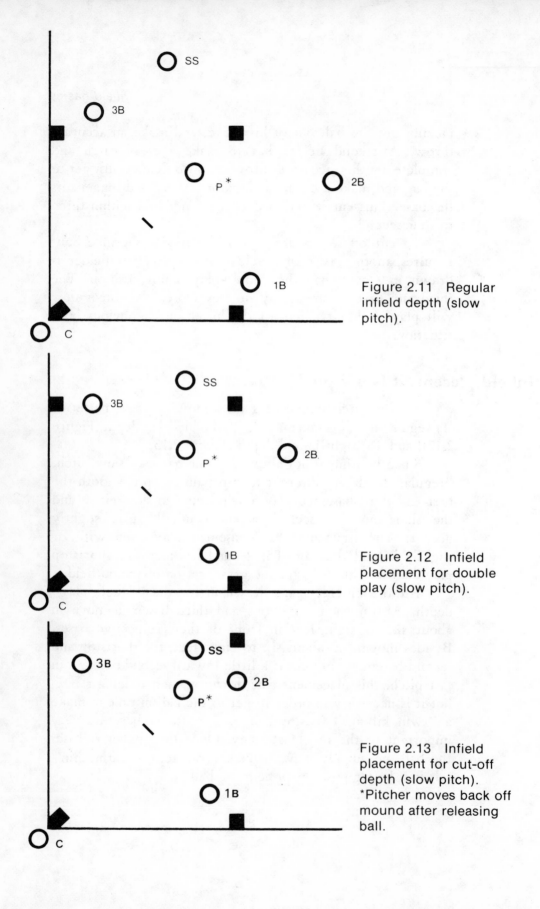

Figure 2.11 Regular infield depth (slow pitch).

Figure 2.12 Infield placement for double play (slow pitch).

Figure 2.13 Infield placement for cut-off depth (slow pitch).
*Pitcher moves back off mound after releasing ball.

When a runner is on third and the run is critical to the outcome of the game, the "tight-infield" depth is used. The first and third basemen move in about five feet in front of the bag, while the shortstop and second baseman move in even with the imaginary base lines going from first to second and second to third. In addition to moving in, both the shortstop and second baseman take a few steps closer to second base. Once again, the pitcher can be a big help in making the play in this situation. By quickly moving back he is in a good spot to field a hot grounder or make a play on a high chopper.

Protecting the foul line

In both fast pitch and slow pitch, the first and third basemen must be alert for hits that may get by them along the foul line. With nobody on base, particularly with one or two out, both the first and third basemen should play a little closer to the foul line than usual. For example, if a hit gets by the third baseman on his right, it usually ends up as an extra-base hit. However, when it gets by him on his left, the shortstop and the left fielder both have a chance to make a stop and hold the hitter to a single.

Photograph by R. Schreul

3

Infield strategy

A fast-pitch infielder has a lot of responsibility and a lot of ground to cover. In addition to handling all kinds of ground balls, line drives, and fly balls, he must be able to handle bunt situations and cover bases in attempted steals. Although the slow-pitch infielder must handle more chances, he does not have to worry about bunts or about protecting the bag from base stealers.

First base (fast pitch)

A first baseman handles the ball more than any other player except the pitcher and catcher. That's why the softball first baseman must be very sure-handed and alert at all times. He or she must play in close for possible bunts and still be able to make a play on sharply hit line drives and ground balls.

Because the first baseman plays close for bunts, he almost always runs back toward the base to receive throws from the other infielders. Therefore, this move should be practiced often by the young player.

When the first baseman sees that a ground ball is heading to another infielder, he immediately runs back to the bag. As soon as he reaches the base, he straddles the bag and faces the infielder making the throw (Figure 3.1). Only after he makes a quick judgment on the height and direction of the throw can he place his feet. If the ball is coming to his right and he is left-handed, he stretches out with his right foot while his left foot touches the outfield corner of the bag. If the throw goes to his left, he makes contact with his left foot on the infield side of the base. This footwork action, which is reversed for a right-handed player (Figure 3.2), gives the first baseman the greatest possible reach.

A good first baseman will come off the base and stop the ball instead of trying to make a spectacular catch of a wild throw. Inexperienced players often try to keep their feet on the bag and stretch for the bad throw. But if the throw pulls the experienced player off the base toward the infield side of

Figure 3.1   First baseman straddles base before throw is made from infielder.

30

Figure 3.2 Stretch by first baseman on ball thrown to infield side of bag. Foot touches inside corner of base.

the bag, he will stay alert and will try to tag the runner on his way to first base.

When and where to play (fast pitch)

In fast pitch the first baseman must play in close, since nearly every hitter could be bunting. With no runners on base and no strike—or one strike—on the batter, play about eight to ten feet in front of first base. After two strikes there is less chance that the hitter will be bunting, and then you can move closer to the bag. Just as in baseball, the hitter will be called out if he bunts foul on the third strike.

Both the third and first basemen play within ten to fifteen feet of the batter in an obvious bunt situation. It's the catcher's job to call out what base the throw should go to after the bunt has been laid down. If the catcher shouts "Second," for example, the first baseman makes the throw to second base. On this type of play a left-handed first baseman has a decided advantage over a right-hander. The left-hander

Figure 3.3   Stretch by first
baseman on ball thrown on outfield
side of bag. Foot touches outside
corner of base.

Figure 3.4   First basemen usually
play behind or even with bag in
slow pitch.

is able to pick up the ball and throw across his body while
the right-hander must make a half turn or even a full turn to
make the play (Figures 3.3, 3.4).

The first baseman plays a little closer to the bag, with
two outs and a right-handed batter at the plate. However, if
a fast left-handed hitter is up, you must play close or else the
hitter may try to drag bunt for a hit.

A slow bouncer that goes between first and second
should be fielded by the first baseman, since he plays much
closer to the hitter. The second baseman will cover first on
this play. The pitcher seldom has time to cover first base in
fast-pitch softball.

Double play (fast pitch)

Although the first baseman plays very close, he must
still be on the watch for a double-play possibility. If a

sharply hit grounder is hit to you, whip the ball to second, which will be covered by the shortstop. Then hustle back to the bag and take the return throw from the shortstop to complete the double play. Sometimes it's impossible for the first baseman to get back to the base after fielding the ball. In this case, an alert second baseman will cover first. The first baseman must be aware of this possibility and keep out of the way of the throw going to first.

A double play may be made with the first baseman touching first base and then throwing to second. In this instance, the runner at second must be tagged out because it is not a force-out.

Second base (fast pitch)

Without a doubt, second base is the most difficult base to play. The second baseman must have all-around skills and make more decisions than any other infielder. One of the most crucial plays, and the main job of the second baseman, is covering first base on a bunt. When an obvious bunt situation arises, you, as second baseman, move a couple of steps closer to first. As soon as the batter turns and faces the pitcher in a bunting position, you should be ready to break for first base. Don't make the mistake of leaving too early just in case the batter decides to hit away.

Once the bunt is put down fairly, dash for first base, keeping your eyes on the play. On some plays you will be able to get to the bag and then take the throw just as a first baseman does. On other plays you may get the throw while you're still on the run, so stay alert all the time. The throw could be coming from either the catcher, pitcher, or first or third baseman.

More ground to cover (fast pitch)

Both the shortstop and second baseman have more ground to cover than any of the other infielders. This is why it's important for the second baseman to be quick on his feet. He should have fast reactions and an accurate throwing arm.

Fielding slow chopped ground balls that are out of the reach of the pitcher and first baseman is a rugged play that the second baseman makes often. Instead of waiting for the easy bounce, you have to charge the ball and take it on the short hop.

As a second baseman, you must sometimes throw the ball in an off-balance position on tough chances that are hit to your extreme left. When fielding balls hit to your extreme left, a backhand snap throw is frequently necessary in order to get the ball to first base in time. Making a play of this type takes a lot of practice and game experience.

Most plays on balls hit to your extreme right will be made with a backhand stop. After making the stop, firmly plant your feet and quickly glance at the runner before you throw. Don't make a hurried throw if there is little chance of getting the runner. An expert infielder can make the backhand pickup and—while still running—jump, turn, and throw in one continuous motion. But this is hard to do and takes time and practice to master.

Double play (fast pitch)

The first and most important move in completing the double play successfully is the throw to the fielder covering the bag (Figure 3.5). An ideal throw is one that reaches the fielder about one or two steps before he steps on the base (Figure 3.6). If the ground ball is hit directly at the second baseman or slightly to his left, he makes a normal sidearm throw to the shortstop covering second. The throw should arrive about waist-high or chest-high. An underhand toss to the shortstop is often used when the ball is hit to the second baseman's extreme right.

When a grounder is hit to the third baseman or short-stop, the second baseman immediately runs toward second

Figure 3.5   Wrong. Ball will get to second baseman too late on double play.

Figure 3.6   Right. Throw will reach fielder one or two steps before he touches second on double play.

base and looks for the throw. The throw should go to the pitcher's side of second base rather than to the outfield side. If the ground ball happens to be hit extremely close to second base, the second baseman will make the double play by fielding the ball, touching second base, and then throwing to first.

Another key move in completing the double play is the pivot at second base. To do this, take the throw and step over the bag with your left foot. As you pass over the base, lightly drag the right foot across the bag. You are then in good position to throw to first base and the baseline is left clear for the runner. Sometimes the double play must be made in such a hurry that it's not possible to place the correct foot on the bag at the right time. If this happens, you must make adjustments and complete the play the best way you can.

Attempted steal (fast pitch)

With a right-handed batter at the plate, the second baseman usually covers second on an attempted steal. The shortstop covers when a left-handed hitter is up. This is not a hard and fast rule, however. Sometimes the second baseman will cover with a left-handed batter at the plate. It depends on who the runner is and what type of hitter is at the plate. Either a hand signal or a verbal code can be used to determine which infielder will cover second base.

There are several moves that must be executed perfectly in order to catch the base stealer. A quick start for the bag by the second baseman is the first one. Keeping a close watch on the runner on every pitch is the secret to getting a quick start. As soon as the runner makes a break toward second, you must dash to second. Watch for the peg from the catcher while running toward the bag. Don't get to the bag and then look for the throw.

A clean catch on the throw, no matter where it's thrown, is the second key move that must be made without a mistake. Even if the throw is off target, a clean catch will give you a chance to tag the runner.

A good infielder moves from the catch to the tag in one smooth motion. The more experienced player makes a one-handed catch and drops the glove to the ground in front of the bag. Young or inexperienced players should use the two-handed catch and then tag the runner with the glove hand.

Shortstop (fast pitch)

Because the shortstop usually makes longer throws than any other infielder, a strong arm is an advantage. This doesn't mean, however, that you need to throw hard on every play. A player with a fair throwing arm, who is able to throw quickly and accurately, can play the shortstop position very well.

Going deep in the hole (between third and deep short) for a ground ball is probably the hardest play a shortstop has

Figure 3.7 Shortstop backhands a ball hit deep in the hole between second and third base.

to make. A backhand stop (Figure 3.7) is normally required to make the catch. Then you must make a long, hard peg in order to get the hitter running to first. This is one of the few times a true overhand throw is recommended. For the most part, the fast-pitch infielder throws sidearm. A sidearm motion allows the infielder to throw more quickly, since he or she doesn't have to straighten up first as when throwing overhand.

When and where to play (fast pitch)

Except when a speedy left-handed batter is up, the shortstop plays fairly deep. Playing deep allows him to cover ground balls hit to his extreme right or left. He can also catch pop flys hit either to short center or left field.

With nobody out and a runner on first, the shortstop has several things to consider. He may have to field ground balls hit in his direction and then throw to the base where he has the best opportunity to get the runner. If the batter bunts, he has to cover second base. He must cover second if the runner tries to steal. He also has to cover second if the ground ball is hit to the pitcher, the second baseman, or the first baseman.

When a sacrifice bunt situation (Figure 3.8) presents itself, the shortstop "cheats" toward second (moves a few steps closer to second base). Once the hitter squares to bunt, start moving cautiously toward second base, keeping your eyes glued on the batter. There is always the possibility the hitter may fake a bunt and then hit away. But once the bunt is down, move quickly to cover second. If the bunt is fielded immediately, the throw usually will be made to second base. Be alert for the possibility of completing a double play. If the bunt has been fielded very fast and a good quick throw has been made to second, it is still possible to get the hitter running to first. Thus, a double play has been completed on an attempted sacrifice bunt; this play that demoralizes your opponents, gives your team a boost.

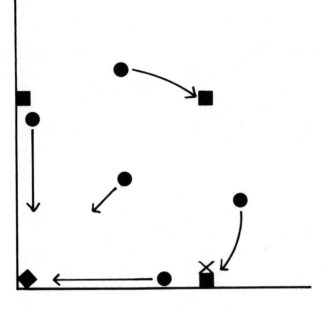

Figure 3.8   This diagram illustrates movement on sacrifice bunt with runner on first only.

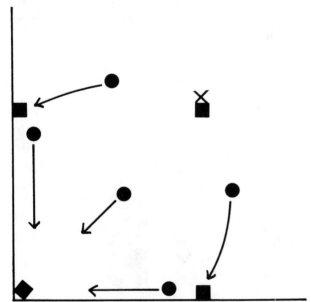

Figure 3.9   Movement of infielders on sacrifice bunt with runner on second or runners on first and second.

If the play is made at first base on a bunt, the shortstop has to leave second immediately and run to cover third. Since the third baseman always charges in on the bunt, he has little chance of getting back in time to cover third. With runners on first and second (Figure 3.9) and nobody out, the short-stop faces a difficult situation. Because it's his job to cover third on either a sacrifice bunt or an attempted double steal, he normally cheats toward third. So if a ball is hit up the center of the diamond, he has to run a long way to make the play.

Double play (fast pitch)

Executing the double play (Figure 3.10) is usually easier for the shortstop than for the second baseman. A second baseman has to make the pivot and then throw back toward first. The shortstop, on the other hand, is running in the same direction he intends to throw.

A good throw hits the shortstop about two steps behind second base on the outfield side of the bag. He then steps over the bag with his left foot and lightly drags the right foot across second base.

Figure 3.10 Beginners practice a double play with actual runner present.

Third base (fast pitch)

Having good hands and the ability to move quickly to your left are the two basic requirements for a third baseman. Since you must play in close on nearly every pitch, quick hands are needed to field hot line drives and sharply hit grounders. Fielding topped grounders that go between the pitcher and the third base foul line is also the third baseman's job. There are two reasons for this. After his delivery, the pitcher is rarely in good position to make a play. Secondly, the shortstop plays too deep to field the ball in time for the putout.

Like the first baseman, the third sacker also has a major job of fielding bunts. In fact, the third baseman usually fields more bunts than any other infielder.

Strategic moves (fast pitch)

There are many special moves required of fast-pitch infielders. During the execution of a defensive move, one small error, either physical or mental, will wreck the play.

Before every pitch, a good infielder will size up the situation and plan what he must do. He must take many things into consideration such as: how many outs there are; what bases are occupied; the hitter's ability; the score; the inning; and the count on the batter.

The following instructions for playing various situations are guidelines only. Remember that each particular game and case may require a little change from the usually recommended way.

Bases empty (fast pitch)

With nobody on base, the first and third basemen play about ten feet in front of the bag. The second baseman and shortstop will play approximately ten to twenty feet behind the imaginary baselines that go from first to second and from second to third.

With a right-handed batter up, the shortstop usually plays a little deeper and about halfway between second and third base. He moves in several steps and takes a position a little closer to second when a left-hander is batting.

The second baseman plays in close and cheats a little toward first base when a left-handed hitter is at the plate. With a right-hander up, the second baseman plays deeper and two or three steps closer to second base.

Bunt

Runner on first (fast pitch)

"Defensing" a sacrifice bunt requires precision timing by all players involved. The moment the batter squares to bunt, both the first and third basemen charge toward home. The second baseman takes a couple of steps closer to first, and the shortstop moves closer to second. Once the bunt is down, the ball will be fielded either by the catcher, first baseman, third baseman, or pitcher. First base will be covered by the second baseman, and second will be covered by the shortstop.

Runners on first and second (fast pitch)

When runners are on first and second, the first and third basemen charge the bunt as usual. First base is covered by the second baseman. The shortstop, however, must cover third on this play. Second base is usually left uncovered.

Runner on second (fast pitch)

With a runner on second only, the first and third basemen charge the bunt. The shortstop covers third base, and the second baseman covers first base. If the play is made at third base, the second baseman must quickly move over to cover second base in case the runner tries to go to second.

Runners on first and third (fast pitch)

Any time a bunt is laid down with a man on third, the infield group have their hands full. When the bunt is dropped, the pitcher and the first and third basemen have to really hustle. Whoever fields the bunt must try to hold the runner on third and still get the runner at first. If the runner makes a serious break for the plate, the infielder scoops up the ball and tosses it with an underhand motion to the catcher, who must make a tag.

On this play the shortstop should cover third base, in case the runner on third gets trapped off base. As usual, the second baseman covers first, and second base is left uncovered. When the second baseman makes the play at first, he has to keep on the watch in case the other runner tries to score after the throw is made to first base.

Outfield hit: bases empty (fast pitch and slow pitch)

Any hit to the outfield involves more movement on the part of the infielders than on the part of the outfielders, who actually field the ball. With no one on base on a single to right field, the following moves take place. The second baseman moves to short right field for a possible relay throw. Second base is covered by the shortstop, and the pitcher moves into the shortstop position to back up the throw (Figure 3.11).

On a hit to center field, either the shortstop or the second baseman will move to short center field for a possible relay throw. Who covers second will depend on where the ball is hit. If it's hit to right center, the shortstop covers second and the pitcher backs up second base (Figure 3.13). When the hit goes to left center, the second baseman covers the bag. The pitcher again becomes the backup man on the throw (Figure 3.14).

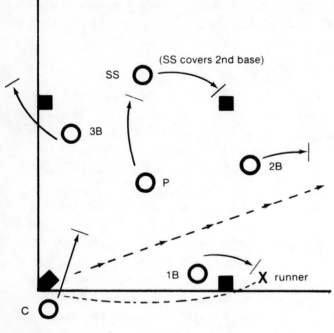

Figure 3.11   Movement of infielders on hit to right field (nobody on).

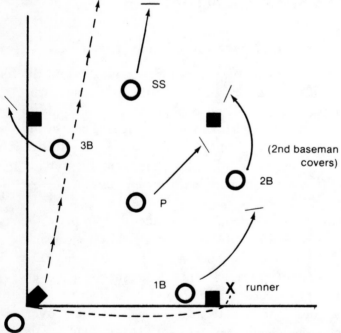

Figure 3.12   Movement of infielders on single to left field (nobody on).

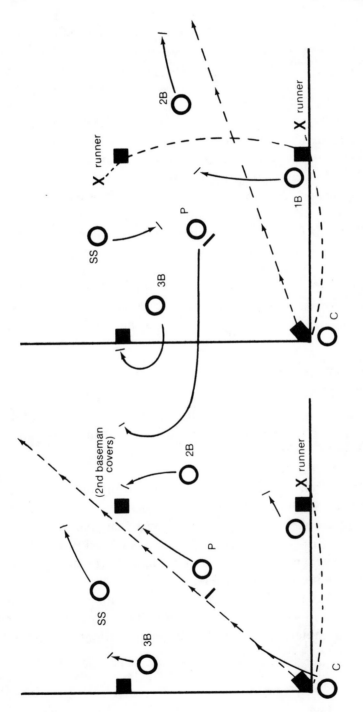

Figure 3.14 Movement of infielder on single to right field (runner on first).

Figure 3.13 Movement of infielders on single to center field (nobody on).

The shortstop moves to short left field on a single to left field, and second base is covered by the second baseman (Figure 3.12). On this play the pitcher is the shallow backup man, and the first baseman is the deep backup player.

On a clean double to the outfield the throw goes to third base, which is always covered by the third baseman. Third base will be backed up by the pitcher. Who will be the relay man will depend on where the ball is hit.

Covering the proper base on a triple is not an easy job. The proper coverage will depend on whether or not the play is going to be close at third base. If it appears that a close play will be made at third, the pitcher backs up the play. On the other hand, the ball may be hit far enough for the runner to try for an inside-the-park home run. At this point, the pitcher has a choice. He may stay at third in the backup position or run and back up the catcher. Some teams prefer to have the first baseman back up the catcher on this play.

First base (slow pitch)

A big, long-ball hitter with average speed and good fielding hands is a good choice for the first base position in slow pitch. His main defensive job is fielding throws on infield putouts.

With the exception of the bunt play (not allowed in slow pitch), all fielding moves and footwork around the bag are the same as those for the fast-pitch first baseman. His regular playing spot is even with the bag or a few feet behind it (Figure 3.14). This position allows the player a better chance of fielding hard line drives and ground balls than being up close where the fast-pitch first baseman plays.

Official rules do not permit the runner to leave the base until the ball reaches home plate. Therefore, the opportunity for completing a double play is excellent, another reason why the first baseman must be a good fielder as well as having a strong, accurate throwing arm.

Second base (slow pitch)

Since there are more hard-hit balls in slow pitch than in fast pitch, the second baseman plays deep. In addition to fielding stinging grounders and line drives, he must put up with chasing short pop-ups (Texas leaguers) hit between infielders and outfielders. Because the outfielders play very deep in slow pitch, there is much open space between the infielders and outfielders.

All of the moves described in the fast-pitch section on making the double play are used by the slow-pitch second sacker. Second base and shortstop are the key positions in the game of slow pitch. These two spots require speed, a good arm, and exceptionally quick hands.

Shortstop (slow pitch)

It's best to be very fast and have an unusually strong arm to be a shortstop in the game of slow pitch. Not only must the shortstop cover a tremendous amount of ground, but he also makes many long and difficult throws. As in the case of the second baseman, the shortstop must be able to get back quickly on short pop flys hit between the infielders and outfielders. Having a strong arm is a big advantage, but throwing accurately with a quick release of the ball is important also.

Third base (slow pitch)

A third baseman normally plays even with the bag or several steps behind it. He should be particularly good at making throws to second base since the chances for force plays and double plays are many in the slow-pitch game. Although most throws from third are made with a sidearm motion in fast pitch, the slow-pitch third sacker throws overhand because of the longer pegs needed.

Outfield relays (slow pitch)

Relays from the outfield are handled by the slow-pitch infield players just as they are in the fast-pitch game. Slow-pitch teams, for the most part, currently use the four-deep outfielder pattern. Because of this, the importance of the second baseman and shortstop as relaymen has increased greatly. Any practice session should have some time devoted to working on the relay play. It is one of the key parts of defensive strategy, yet it is usually the most neglected.

Outfield hit: bases occupied (fast pitch and slow pitch)

When only first base is occupied, infield strategy is fairly easy. On a single to the outfield, the throw should immediately go to third base. Third base will be covered by the third baseman, with the pitcher backing up the play.

If more than one base is occupied, movement of the infielders depends on the situation. The inning, score of the game, how far the ball is hit, and the runner's speed all play a role in where the throw will go and where the fielders move. Regardless of where the play is made, someone should be backing up the throw.

Slow-pitch strategy

Except for playing the bunt and covering on the steal,

information in this chapter also applies to the slow-pitch infielders. Backing up bases, making the double play, and moving to the proper base after a hit to the outfield require almost the same moves in slow pitch as in fast pitch. The main difference is the placement of the infielders.

4

The outfielder

A fast-pitch outfielder doesn't get nearly the action the other players do. But any mistake he makes is extremely costly. An infielder who lets the ball get through him usually lets a runner get an extra base. However, if an outfielder allows the ball to get past him, the runner may take at least two extra bases. Throwing quickly and accurately is more important than having a strong arm. Furthermore, the fast pitch outfielder doesn't have to be extremely fast.

A left fielder and right fielder can have average speed, but it's best if the center fielder is a good, fast man who can make quick, accurate throws. Since there are not too many hits that go into the outfield in fast pitch, a player who is an excellent hitter but only an average fielder has a good chance of playing the outfield. Many fine outfield players are neither fast nor do they have a great arm.

Outfield flyballs

Judging a flyball is a skill that is not easily taught. Being a good outfielder comes through hard work and long hours of practice. For example, a hard, low, line drive hit directly at the fielder is probably one of the most difficult plays to make in the outfield. Getting a jump on the ball is a big advantage in the outfield. But on the low line drive you must be careful. The natural instinct of the fielder is to come in fast on the low liner. The line drive often starts low and looks as if it's coming directly at the fielder, but sometimes it continues to rise and often goes over his head for extra bases.

An outfielder handles a pop fly just as the infielder does, but he deals with much longer hit balls. A pop fly that is hit high enough for the outfield to camp under is fairly easy to make. Yet, during a day game when there is a bright sun, it's very easy to be temporarily blinded and lose the ball. Losing the ball will sometimes happen during a night game when the outfielder looks directly into the lights.

Learning to shade your eyes and not lose sight of the ball is a big factor in making the catch in the outfield. An experienced outfielder will watch the ball from the moment it comes off of the bat until it's right in his glove. It's a big mistake for an outfielder to panic when he temporarily loses sight of the ball.

A job that all outfielders must learn is to go back on long fly balls. As soon as he determines a ball is going to drive him back, he must turn, run, and catch the ball over his shoulder. You go after this type of fly ball very much as you would catch a football on a forward pass. One thing you must never do is back-pedal (Figure 4.1) when trying to make the catch on a long fly ball. The outfield area is seldom as smooth as the infield. So it's doubly important to get in front of the ground ball to keep it from going under your glove. To keep the runner from getting an extra base, the outfielder should always be charging the ground ball (Figure 4.2). Any slight bobble or delay will allow a fast runner to stretch a single into a double. The outfielder should both reach the ball quickly, and get rid of it as quickly as possible.

Figure 4.1   Never back pedal on long fly ball. Ball is caught over the shoulder like a football pass.

Figure 4.2   Outfielder must charge ground balls.

Always throw to the lead base, never behind the runner. Throwing behind the runner means that you're throwing to the base the runner has already rounded. Clever base runners often go past the base to "sucker" the outfielder into throwing behind them. Once the outfielder throws, the runner takes off for the next base. It's seldom possible to get a runner by throwing behind him. Always play it safe and throw to the lead base.

Throwing from the outfield

Throws from the outfield should be made with an overhand motion (Figure 4.3). Throwing overhand keeps the ball from curving, which may happen when you throw sidearm. A deep throw from the outfield to home plate should bounce once before it reaches the catcher. This type of throw is handled more easily if it hits the ground about ten to fifteen feet in front of home plate. The catcher has a

Figure 4.3 Outfielder makes throws with overhand motion.

better chance of making the tag if the throw is slightly toward the third base side of home.

A ball that gets past an outfielder or goes between two outfielders must be quickly retrieved by the first fielder who can get to it. A quick and accurate throw must then be made to a relay man. This throw is the most important part of the relay play. It should reach the relay man about waist- or chest-high on the fly. Any throw that is too low or one that makes the infielder jump causes a slight delay. A fraction of a second may be all that is needed for a runner to take an extra base.

When and where to play

In general, a fast-pitch outfielder plays much more shallow than the baseball or slow-pitch outfielder. Since the pitcher in fast pitch is so effective, a good share of the balls hit to the outfield are pop flies and short singles. Consequently, the center fielder plays closer than either one of the other outfielders. His job is to catch the short pop-fly hit behind the shortstop and the second baseman as well as the longer line drives and fly balls.

Such things as the number of outs, runners on base, the hitter, score of the game, type of field, and inning, have an effect on where the outfielders will play. For example, when there's a good long ball hitter up with two out and nobody on, the entire outfield can afford to play deep. But if a runner on third represents the winning run and it's the bottom half of the last inning with less than two outs, the entire outfield plays extremely close. Any hit in the outfield or a long fly ball will end the game.

With the outfielders playing in close, there is a good chance to hold the runner on a short pop fly. In some cases it's even possible to throw him out at the plate on a ground ball hit. Outfielders in this position also have a good chance of making a play on a low, sinking line drive that would normally fall in for a hit.

Right fielder

Backing up throws going to first base is a key responsibility of the right fielder. Because there are many bunts in fast pitch, the right fielder must always be ready to back up first. As soon as the right fielder sees a hitter square around to bunt, he moves in toward the foul line in case of an overthrow.

It's the right fielder's job to back up the center fielder on any hits to right center field. Since the center fielder is usually playing in close, the right fielder must always be alert for balls that get through and go to the fence. Even when the center fielder is camped underneath a pop fly toward right center, the right fielder should quickly run over just in case the center fielder loses the ball in the sun or misjudges the ball.

On a single to right field with nobody on, the right fielder charges the ball and throws to second base. A single to right field with first base occupied requires a throw to third base. This throw is fairly long, and a one-bounce peg is a better choice than trying to throw it on the fly.

A hit to right with a runner on second means the throw should go to second base. This play holds the runner on first. Unless the base runner represents a winning run in the late innings, the ball should always be thrown to second base on this play. It's almost impossible for a right fielder to throw a runner out at the plate unless he's pulled in very, very close.

A hit that gets past the right fielder usually means that a relay throw is necessary. The second baseman is the relay man on hits to right field (Figure 4.4). Remember, it's vital to get the ball quickly and make an accurate throw to the relay man. Don't be too hasty and try to pick up the ball too fast. It's particularly important when you consider that the ball is often wet during night games. Grasp the ball firmly before making the throw. Again, throwing quickly and accurately to the relay man is better than hurrying and trying to make a hard throw that misses him.

An inexperienced outfielder will go after the ball and

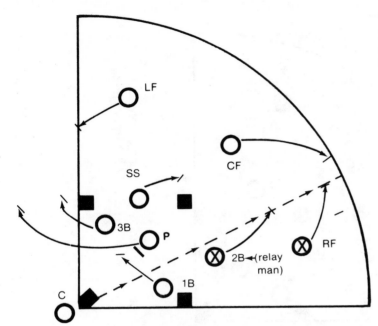

Figure 4.4 Relay positions of infielders and outfielders on extra-base hit to right field.

then try to see how the play is developing. The best policy is to quickly pick up the ball and immediately look for your relay man.

Center fielder

A center fielder should be the most versatile player in the outfield. He plays more shallow than the other out-fielders, but he still must be able to go back fast on long fly balls. He should be quick, capable of fielding ground balls well, and have a good, accurate arm.

A center fielder is in a good position to see the ball come off the bat. As a result, he can come in extremely fast on short hits to center. Most throws he makes to either the second or third basemen are on the fly.

On some occasions the center fielder may have to go into deep right center on an extra-base hit (Figure 4.5). In this case, the throw to third may call for a one-bounce peg, just as you would normally make to home.

All suggestions given for the right fielder on throwing

57

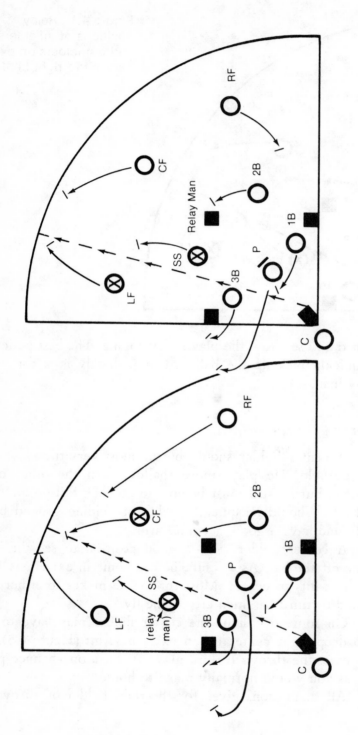

Figure 4.6 Relay positions of infielders and outfielders on extra-base hit to left field.

Figure 4.5 Relay position of infielders and outfielders on extra-base hit to center field.

to the relay man also apply to the center fielder. One exception is the relay man. On a ball hit to deep right center, the relay man is the second baseman. The shortstop will be the relay man on hits to center and left center field. With a runner on second, a center fielder usually has the best chance to throw out a runner at home on a short single to the outfield. Whether to throw to home or to second is best learned through game experience.

Left fielder

Besides backing up the center fielder, one of the main jobs of the left fielder is to back up third base. Since the shortstop often moves over to cover third on bunts and steals, and because this is a difficult play, overthrows are quite common.

A left fielder usually has more action than the right fielder because there are more right-handed hitters. He should be able to come in on ground balls quickly and have good fielding hands. He doesn't have to make the long throw to third, and consequently a fielder with an average arm can play left field comfortably.

On short hits to the outfield, the left fielder throws the ball on the fly to the infielders covering either second or third base.

On an extra-base hit, the relay man for the left fielder is the shortstop (Figure 4.6). A left fielder plays in closer to third base than the other fielders, so it is sometimes better to make the throw directly to third base rather than use the shortstop. The shortstop or center fielder will usually shout instructions as to where the ball should be thrown.

Before the game

Prior to the start of the game, outfielders should carefully check the field for bumps, bare spots, or any other unusual characteristics that may affect his play. During the regular season, bare spots are worn in the grass where the outfielder stands. These spots often become bumpy. Ground balls will take unusually bad hops when they hit this portion of the field. An alert fielder will always try to charge a ground ball and make the pickup before it reaches these bare spots. During these outfield checks, it's a good idea to look for light poles and other obstructions. Foul flies may be hit near light poles, dugouts, or even trees. Running into such an obstacle might not only lose the ball game, it could be the cause of serious injury.

Always get a feel for how far back you can go without running into the outfield fence. Fields are constructed in different ways and often have varying distances to the outfield fences. Check the amount of room you have from the foul line to the bleachers or foul line fence (Figure 4.7).

Warm-up periods are valuable for checking the brightness and location of the sun before day games. It's a good idea for the person hitting balls during the outfield drill to hit ground balls as well as fly balls. This gives the outfielders a chance to check field conditions and dampness of the grass.

Slow-pitch outfield

Outfielders in slow pitch must be extremely fast and excellent fielders. A slow-pitch outfielder does all the things required of a fast-pitch outfielder, and he does them more often. Slow-pitch teams play two basic patterns in their outfield strategy. Some play with a short center fielder and three deep outfielders, while others play with four deep outfielders (Figure 4.8). Apparently, the four-deep strategy is most common in slow pitch. Long, low line drives and short pop flies can drop for hits with this type of outfield, however. Nevertheless, as slow-pitch hitters have improved over the years, long, low hard line drives have become the rule, not the exception. Playing four deep outfielders seems to be the best way of reducing the number of total base hits. Instructions that were given for fast-pitch outfielders also apply for slow pitch. This includes throwing, fielding, and

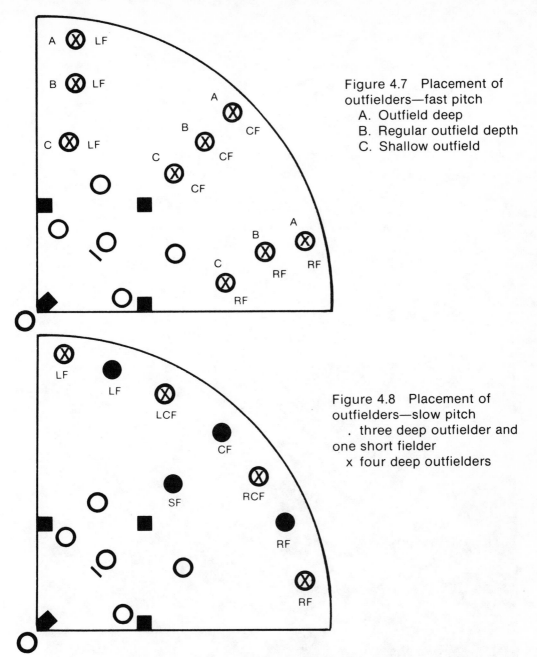

Figure 4.7 Placement of outfielders—fast pitch
A. Outfield deep
B. Regular outfield depth
C. Shallow outfield

Figure 4.8 Placement of outfielders—slow pitch
. three deep outfielder and one short fielder
x four deep outfielders

backing up other outfielders and infielders. Actually, slow-pitch outfielders are not concerned with backing up bases on bunts or steals. They always play deeper than the fast-pitch outfielders. It's not an easy job to hit good pitching in the game of fast pitch. First of all, the pitcher is closer and the ball gets to the plate faster than it does in baseball. Since a softball has a greater surface area than a baseball, the softball tends to break considerably more.

5

The pitcher

As far as technique is concerned, there is a great deal of difference between the pitcher in fast pitch and the slow-pitch chucker. In fast pitch the actual delivery of the ball closely resembles the pitching delivery used in baseball. Actually, the delivery for fast pitch is a throwing motion, whereas the slow-pitch delivery is a slow, easy, tossing motion similar to pitching horseshoes or rolling a bowling ball.

Because there is such a big difference between the two techniques, the first portion of this chapter will be devoted to fast pitch. The second part of the chapter will contain the fundamentals for pitching slow pitch.

Attitude

A pitcher must develop the proper attitude to go along with his or her physical maturity. Maintaining a calm and even temperament is a tremendous asset to any pitcher.

Pitching a complete game is not an easy job. In addition to the physical energy used, mental stress caused by errors can affect performance. If you can take an error in stride without letting it bother your concentration, you'll be on the way to becoming a mature chucker. Teasing and taunts by opponents and spectators must be brushed aside. Calls by an umpire may even seem unfair or incorrect. Once you are capable of facing these conditions calmly, you have overcome a big hurdle in becoming a consistent winner. If an opponent discovers that you become upset, he will use this weakness to his advantage in future games.

Another important characteristic is self-confidence. You have to believe in yourself. Even if you have a bad game and get knocked around, tell yourself it's just one of those days. Be ready to come back and do your best the next time out.

Desire and dedication round out the list of a good pitcher's required traits. Any goal of importance is reached only with hard work. To become a good fast-pitch chucker, you need desire, dedication, and hard work. It means practicing nearly every day for several years besides playing in pick-up games and organized leagues.

Proper stance

Just like an infielder and an outfielder, a pitcher must start by learning the fundamentals. The first step is to learn the proper stance on the mound. First, the pitcher places both feet firmly on the ground and in contact with the pitching rubber (Figure 5.1). Neither foot may be at the side of the rubber. Before throwing the ball, a pitcher must come to a complete stop and face the batter. This phase is known as a presentation stance. Shoulders are in line with first and third base and the ball is held in both hands in front of the body. The ball must be presented for at least one second but no longer than 20 seconds before the windup begins.

Figure 5.1 Pitcher places both feet firmly on the ground, in contact with the pitching rubber (fast ptich).

Regulation pitch

The regulation pitch begins as soon as the hand is taken off the ball. A pitcher is allowed only one stride or step and it must be forward and toward the batter. The rear foot must stay on the pitching rubber until the ball is released. Keeping the rear foot on the pitching rubber is an important part of fast pitch. Some pitchers have a bad habit of sliding their rear foot off the mound to get extra momentum on the pitch. Unfortunately, once this habit has been developed over a period of time, it's hard to correct. Even though some pitchers get away with this for several years, one never knows when an umpire will call it an illegal pitch. Usually an umpire will issue a warning, but once the error is repeated, he will call a ball on every pitch. This is termed an illegal pitch. On an illegal pitch all runners automatically advance one base.

Proper delivery

In a legal delivery the ball is pitched to the batter with an underhand motion. Both the release of the ball and the follow-through of the hand and wrist must be forward, past the straight line of the body. When the arm passes the line of the body, the hand must be below the hip and the wrist no farther from the body than the elbow is (Figure 5.2). But, the wrist and hand may be away from the elbow before passing the line of the body. Extension of the wrist and hand beyond the elbow before passing the body is how "stuff" in fast pitch

Figure 5.2 As arm passes the line of the body, hand must be below the hip and the wrist no further from the body than the elbow.

(throwing curves, rise balls, drops, etc.) is put on the ball.

Windup (fast pitch)

As long as it meets the following rules, any windup can be used by the pitcher.
1. A motion to pitch cannot be made without pitching the ball.
2. Only one complete revolution of the arm is permitted.
3. A rocker motion is not permitted.

A rocker motion will be called by the umpire if the pitcher is holding the ball with both hands in the presentation position and then removes one hand from the ball, makes a backward and then forward swing and brings the ball to both hands again. This violation will be called an illegal pitch.

Pitching rubber

An official pitching rubber is 24 inches long and 6 inches wide. It should be made from wood or rubber and the top must be level with the ground. The official pitching distance for men's fast pitch, men's slow pitch, and women's slow pitch is 46 feet. Official distance of women's fast pitch is 40 feet.

It's good for the young pitcher to practice with an official pitching rubber. Sometimes a beginner practices on plain ground and then finds it difficult to pitch off a rubber during the game. As a beginning pitcher, you need not be too concerned about control and speed. You should develop a comfortable and smooth delivery before worrying about anything else. After many, many hours and days of practicing a delivery, then you may concentrate on speed and control.

One of the best ways to improve control is to throw with an actual batter standing in the box. Although it's helpful to practice with just the catcher present, a beginner should have a batter present often. Also, it's good for the batter to stand on both sides of the plate. If you can't find a batter, place a chair or box in the batter's box.

Warming up (fast pitch)

Regardless of your age, the game, or your pitching style, a consistent warm-up before practice or a game is a must. It not only prepares you for the game, but it prevents a sore arm or even a permanent injury. Each pitcher develops his own routines, but it's a good idea to start by jogging a few minutes. In some cases, wind sprints are helpful, particularly in the early part of the season. Wear a jacket during the first portion of the routine. The jacket will hold the heat generated by jogging and help to warm up muscles and ligaments.

Actual pitching completes the warm-up period. Start by merely tossing the ball easily, both underhand and overhand. This loosens up many of the muscles of the forearm, upper arm, and back. After a few minutes, throw at half speed without putting any stuff on the ball. Always use your regular windup, delivery, and follow-through during warm-up, and throw from the regulation distance.

After throwing at half speed, start throwing stuff and concentrate on one pitch only. Slowly increase your speed until you're throwing wide open. Follow the same routine when you switch to another type of pitch. After you've gone through your entire assortment of pitches, begin to mix them as you would in a game.

Pitching style (fast pitch)

For a beginner between the ages of 12 and 16, it's best to settle on a style that is comfortable. The two basic styles are the windmill and the slingshot. Regardless of what style is used, both deliveries require the same action as the sidearm or overhand baseball pitching motion. An underhand delivery in fast pitch is a throwing motion and is not like tossing horseshoes or rolling a bowling ball.

Slingshot

Before anything else, find a comfortable stance on the rubber. A right-hander, for example, usually places his right foot slightly forward of his left foot. The toe is placed in front of the rubber, with the heel making contact with the rubber. Pitchers vary considerably in where they place the rear foot. Ordinarily, the rear foot rests about four to six inches behind the front foot. The toe portion of the shoe

Figure 5.3   Slingshot delivery sequence: (A) drop pitching arm downward and backward.

Figure 5.4   (B) At furthest point of backswing, extend front leg.

Figure 5.5   (C) Plant foot firmly   Figure 5.6   (D) Release ball.
and snap arm forward.

makes contact with the back of the rubber. How far the feet
are spread sideways depends upon individual preference.

   With both the slingshot and the windmill, the pitcher
begins the windup with both hands holding the ball in front
of the body. At the very start of the slingshot motion, the
pitching hand holding the ball is dropped downward and
backward (Figure 5.3). This motion is continued until the
hand is behind and above the head (Figure 5.4). As the
pitching hand is drawn from the glove, lean forward with
knees slightly bent. At the point where the pitcher's arm is at
the farthest point of the backswing, the front leg will be
fully extended (Figure 5.5). The arm is then snapped forward

and the front foot is planted firmly on the ground just before the ball is released (Figure 5.6).

Windmill

A windmill delivery begins with the pitcher in the regular presentation position. As the pitching hand is brought out of the glove (Figure 5.7), the upper portion of the body is bent slightly forward. Knees are also slightly bent in preparation for the forward stride. The pitching arm is then raised above the head as the circular motion starts (Figure 5.8). At the very top of the motion the arm is bent slightly at the elbow (Figure 5.9). This cocked-wrist action creates the

Figure 5.7　Windmill delivery sequence: (A) At start of windup, draw pitching hand out of glove and bend slightly forward.

Figure 5.8　(B) Raise pitching arm above head, starting the circular motion.

Figure 5.9   (C) Bend arm slightly
at the very top of the circular
motion.

Figure 5.10   (D) Continue forward
stride as arm moves in the circle.

speed and the stuff required of the fast pitch windmill
delivery. While the arm moves in a complete circular motion, the forward stride continues. (Figure 5.10). When the
ball is released, the striding foot is planted firmly (Figure
5.11). The length of time the rear foot remains in contact
with the pitching rubber can vary. In some cases the rear
foot is lifted almost simultaneously with the release of the
ball, yet other pitchers leave the rear foot in contact with the
rubber after the release of the ball.

Pitching assortment

Although there are exceptions, it is very difficult for a

Figure 5.11   (E) Release ball and plant forward foot.

youngster to throw stuff before the teen years. When the young, fast-pitch chucker is ready to throw curves, rise balls, and drops, there is a very important point to consider. There is no one way to grip the ball for a certain pitch. Proper rotation is more important than how the ball is held. A ball will break the way the ball is rotated when it leaves the pitcher's hand. The amount of break will depend on the speed of rotation (spin) and how hard the ball is thrown.

Drop ball

A drop ball has a downward spin. If you're standing between the pitcher's mound and home plate toward the third base foul line, the ball would have a clockwise spin (Figure 5.12). An easy way to get the downward spin is to let the ball roll off the end of your fingers. Most pitchers grip the drop ball across the seams (Figure 5.13). Some grip the

73

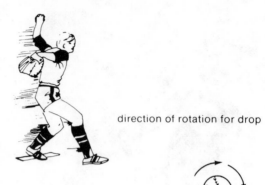

direction of rotation for drop

Figure 5.12   Rotation of
drop is clockwise
(viewed from third base
foul line).

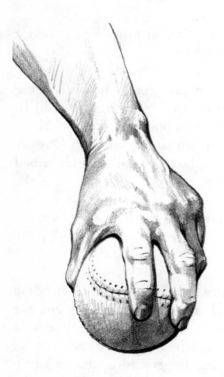

Figure 5.13   A typical grip for
throwing drop ball.

Figure 5.14   Another grip for
throwing drop ball.

ball with two fingers, some with three, and others with four
(Figure 5.14).

In-shoot

An in-shoot is sometimes called a screwball. The in-shoot is also thrown by letting the ball roll off the end of the fingertips, similar to the drop. However, the fingers are more in a perpendicular plane to the ground when the ball is released.

Rise ball

As the arm is brought forward on the downward part of the delivery, the wrist should be in a cocked position. The hand is cupped, the wrist is bent and extended outward out beyond the forearm. The wrist is then snapped just before it passes the line of the body. At this point the wrist, forearm, and hand are a straight line passing parallel to the body. During the follow-through motion, the wrist continues to turn. This snap of the wrist makes the ball spin in an upward

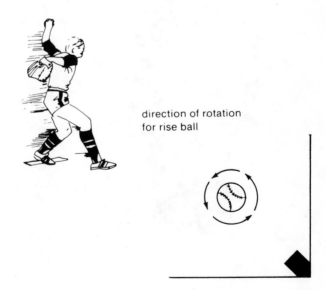

direction of rotation
for rise ball

Figure 5.15 Rotation of
rise is counterclockwise
(viewed from third base
foul line.)

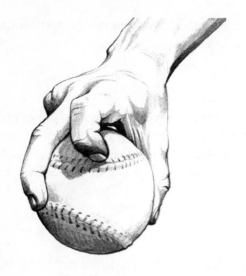

Figure 5.16   One method for gripping rise ball.

Figure 5.17   Another way of gripping the rise ball.

Figure 5.18   Still another way of gripping rise ball.

direction. If you were observing the ball from the third base foul line, the ball would be spinning in a counterclockwise direction (Figure 5.15).

Many different grips (Figures 5.17 and 5.18) are used for throwing the rise ball. The majority of pitchers tuck or bend one finger against the seam (Figure 5.16), or even place the knuckle on the ball. The straighter the back spin, the more the ball will rise. Always keep in mind that a drop goes off the fingertips, whereas the rise and curve balls roll off the sides of the fingers.

Curve

A curve is gripped and thrown in a similar way to the rise ball. On the curve, the wrist is extended and cupped more just before the release of the ball. The wrist is rotated much the same as the rise ball. However, on the follow-through motion, the wrist and hand move slightly across the front of the body. A curve normally is intended to move away from the batter.

Change-up

A change of pace pitch (change-up) may be a slow drop, a slow rise, or a slow curve. Change-ups are thrown to keep a batter off balance. The key to a good change of pace is a consistent delivery. Your release of the ball, windup, and delivery have to look the same as all of your other pitches. To throw a good change-up, the speed of the ball must be slower than your other pitches. This must be accomplished without changing your regular motion.

The fielding pitcher

As fast-pitch chuckers mature in their pitching ability, they often neglect their fielding responsibilities. A good coach or manager can prevent this from happening by including the pitcher in infield drills during practice. It's also a good idea for the young pitcher to play other infield positions so his or her fielding skills won't slip.

One of the toughest jobs for the pitcher is covering the bunt. When the pitcher fields a bunt, he usually throws to a fielder who is moving toward the base to cover. Therefore, it's best to practice this under game conditions. Base runners should be used whenever possible.

You must charge the bunt quickly, but not so fast that you overrun it. A bunt may be spinning as it comes off a bat and may move in any direction. Charge the bunt with feet well spread so you can quickly change your direction. Use the same approach for fielding and throwing as the infielder. These techniques are described in Chapter 3, "Infield Strategy." As you pick up the bunt, listen for the catcher, who will tell you where the throw should go.

Backing up

Backing up the proper base is one job often neglected by the pitcher. Failure to back up bases can be traced to a lack of basic fundamentals. A drill to teach proper techniques for backing up bases should be included in every practice session. Although the pitcher must back up all the bases, third base is the most important. Other bases can be backed up by other infielders, but third base is the pitcher's responsibility. How and when to back up the base is included in Chapter 3.

Pitching—slow pitch

Starting with the basics of pitching in slow pitch is just as important as in fast pitch even though the rules are less complicated. The pitcher takes a position with one foot firmly on the ground and in contact with the pitching rubber.

Your foot may touch the front, middle, or rear portion of the rubber, but it can't be in contact with the side of the rubber.

Before pitching, your arm must come to a complete stop and you must hold the ball in front of the body. This position must be held for at least one second but not more than 20 seconds before releasing the ball. The ball must be pitched toward home plate on the first forward swing of the pitching arm. Any pitch begins when the pitcher makes a motion that is a part of the windup (Figure 5.19). No stop or reverse motion is permitted.

After the delivery is begun, the pivot foot must stay on the rubber until the ball leaves the pitcher's hand. There is

Figure 5.19 Slow pitch delivery sequence: (A) Begin pitch with windup.

Figure 5.20 (B) Deliver pitch underhand.

Figure 5.21 (C) Aim for an arc range of at least three feet.

Figure 5.22 (D) There is no limit on the height of the pitch.

no rule on the positioning of the feet, but if a step is taken, it must be made at the same time the ball is pitched. After the ball is released, the pitcher may move in any direction.

A legal pitch is one that is delivered underhand with the arm passing below the hips (Figure 5.20). Each pitch must have an arc range of at least three feet from the time it leaves the pitcher's hand (Figure 5.21) until it crosses home plate. There is no limit on the height of the pitch (Figure 5.22). It must be delivered at a moderate speed. The umpire will warn the pitcher if he judges the speed to be too fast. Should the fast pitch be repeated, the umpire removes the pitcher from the game.

Tape or any other substance is not allowed on the pitching hand or fingers. No foreign substance can be put on the ball at any time. The pitcher may use powdered rosin to dry the hands, however. Pitchers cannot wear sweatbands, bracelets, or similar items on the wrist or forearm of the pitching arm.

Fielding

Since the game of slow pitch was created for plenty of hitting action, the pitcher in slow pitch must be a good fielder. A good fielding pitcher is able to make many key assists. Because there are many base hits in the game, the pitcher is very important as a backup man. Backing up bases also is covered in Chapter 3, "Infield Strategy."

Pitching technique

Pitchers in fast pitch have a great advantage over the hitter. In slow pitch, the batter has the greater advantage. But, the pitcher in slow pitch has little opportunity to fool the hitter. One way the pitcher keeps the hitter off-balance is to vary the height of the pitching arc. The higher the pitcher makes the arc, the more difficult the angle of contact for hitting the ball becomes. However, the higher the pitcher "arcs" the ball, the more difficult it becomes to throw strikes.

Although the rules prevent the pitcher from throwing rise balls, curve balls, etc., he can put backspin on the ball. Backspin can be thrown by releasing the ball with the back of the hand upward and rolling the ball off the tips of the fingers. When the pitcher learns to throw strikes consistently with a very high arc, it is good to throw a backspin pitch once in a while. Some pitchers are able to throw backspin balls on every pitch. As the pitcher becomes more skilled, he can vary the height of the arc with backspin as well as placing the ball on the inside and outside corners of the plate.

Finer points

A proper and consistent warm-up at the regular pitching distance is something the pitcher in slow pitch should consider. You should also use the same presentation and delivery during the warm-up as you would in the actual game.

Knowing the hitters' weaknesses is as important in slow pitch as in fast pitch. Although as a pitcher, you don't have the chance to throw a great variety of pitches, you can aim for certain spots. If a hitter has trouble hitting an outside pitch solidly, take advantage of that weakness.

Pitching strategy does differ somewhat from that of fast pitch. In slow pitch, the pitcher sometimes throws to the batter's strength. For example, a batter who pulls the ball likes an inside pitch. Sometimes the pitcher throws to this strength. The fielders will then overshift in that direction.

As soon as the pitcher releases the ball, he quickly moves back. By watching where the pitch goes (inside or outside of the plate) he moves in the direction he thinks the batter will hit the ball. Too often the importance of the pitcher is overlooked. Not only can he or she be a valuable asset for pitching, but also, this fielding can make the difference between an average infield and a very good infield unit.

Photograph by R. Schreul

6

The catcher

A catcher in fast pitch has more responsibility than any other player. He or she should be a leader, a take-charge person who can put pep into the entire team when it's needed most. It's the catcher's responsibility to call the pitches and remind teammates how many outs there are. A good memory is needed in order to recall all hitters' weaknesses and to know how well the pitcher can handle each hitter.

Other responsibilities of the catcher include: positioning outfielders and calling out the base that the ball should go to on a bunt situation. In addition, he or she usually makes the decision as to when the ball should be cut off on throws from the outfield. As a catcher, you should be a student of the rule books since you are involved in nearly every play in the ball game.

Although catchers come in all sizes and shapes, it's advisable to be strong, tough, and limber. The catcher in fast pitch is likely to be subjected to more injuries than anyone else on the field. Catchers frequently have to face hard slides at the plate and are often hit by stinging foul tips. It's a distinct advantage to have a good, strong arm, but it's not absolutely necessary. It's more important to have a good, accurate arm and to be able to get rid of the ball quickly. A catcher doesn't need outstanding speed but must be able to move very fast in any direction.

Proper stance

Being comfortable in the proper stance is one of the first steps to becoming a good catcher. The typical stance, which is a combination of a squat and a crouch (Figure 6.1), allows a catcher to stop balls in the dirt, move out quickly for bunts or topped ground balls, and handle both high and low pitches.

A young catcher often makes the mistake of standing too far behind the batter. Consequently, he has trouble fielding low pitches that hit in front of him.

Besides standing too far away from the batter, the

Figure 6.1 Typical stance for receiving pitch.

inexperienced catcher often blinks his eyes when the batter swings. This is a very common mistake and is nothing to worry about. Eventually this problem will disappear through regular practice and playing experience.

An experienced catcher stands close to the batter with his feet spread comfortably. Weight is placed on the balls of the feet, allowing easy movement in either direction. In this position, he or she can turn quickly for a foul fly as well as get ready to throw to any base.

Giving the signal

Signals are given to the pitcher by the catcher in a squat position. Signals, or signs as they're sometimes called, are flashed with the fingers of the throwing hand. When there are no runners on base, signals can be kept simple. For example, one finger can mean a drop; two fingers, a curve; three fingers, a rise, and so on. But when second base is occupied, it's a good idea to have a code so that the runner

Figure 6.2 Signals are given with fingers of throwing hand. Catcher's mitt is used to hide signals from third base coach.

won't steal the signals and flash them to a coach or the batter. A simple code could be a prearranged series of signals. Another method includes using a key sign.

In some cases the first signal flashed is the key that determines which sign of the series is the right one. If one finger is flashed on the first signal, or key sign, the pitch wanted will be given on the very next signal in the series. When two fingers are flashed on the first signal, or key sign, it indicates the intended signal will be given on the second signal after the key.

Signals should be given to the pitcher with fingers placed very deep in the crotch area (Figure 6.2). If the fingers are held too low, the sign could be picked up by

Figure 6.3 Clenched fingers on throwing hand prevent injury from foul tips.

Figure 6.4 Catcher must get body in front of balls that bounce in the dirt.

either the first or third base coach. There are other ways that a catcher might sometimes give away a signal. Some catchers hold the glove high on the rise and low on the drop when presenting a target. This makes it easy for the coach to steal the signal.

Receiving the pitch

When the pitcher is ready to throw, the catcher holds the glove up and open, providing a clear target for the pitcher. The fingers of the throwing hand should be slightly clenched and held behind the thumb portion of the glove (Figure 6.3). In this manner the catcher prevents broken fingers from foul tips or wild pitches.

Once the ball hits the glove, the throwing hand quickly slides over the ball, keeping it in the pocket of the glove. There are two types of pitches that give the catcher trouble with the players on base. One is a pitch that bounces in the dirt directly in front of the catcher (Figure 6.4). The other is an inside pitch that looks as if it will hit the batter; in this case, the hitter's body actually screens the ball, and the catcher may temporarily lose sight of the pitch. In either instance the catcher must do his best to get his body in front of the ball to keep it from going back to the screen.

Pop fly

Getting the mask off quickly (Figure 6.5) is the first step in going for a pop fly. Not only should the mask come off quickly, but it should be thrown aside. Otherwise the catcher may stumble over the mask. Many times the pop fly can be extremely high, and wind can carry it a long distance. A good catcher always keeps the ball in front of him in order to keep from back-pedaling. Back-pedaling after the ball is often the reason that the catcher drops pop flies.

Figure 6.5   Getting mask off
quickly is first step in going after
pop-up.

Protecting the plate

Any game can be decided on one final play at home
plate. Making that play properly is not easy, even for the
most experienced catcher. Throws from the outfield, for
example, often come in on a bounce and take a bad hop. In
addition, the runner trying to score will be giving everything
he or she has and the catcher must be ready to take a hard
knock. First and foremost, the catcher must make a clean
catch of the throw and at the same time keep one eye on the
runner to determine to what side of the plate he is heading.
An inexperienced catcher often takes his eyes off the ball and
looks at the runner. Once he does that, he has a hard time
making a clean catch. He is unlikely to have a good enough
grip to hold on to the ball making the tag.

Some catchers try to block the plate with their body to
keep the runner from scoring. Sometimes they may get away
with it, but this is a dangerous practice. In addition, the

umpire has the right to rule interference and call the runner safe. The best way to block the plate is to make a clean catch of the ball, hold it tightly in your glove in front of the plate, and allow the runner to slide into the tag.

Whether a runner comes in standing up or sliding, it's best to make the tag while in the crouch, with the feet straddling the plate. The glove hand should grasp the ball tightly, held well in front of the plate and on the ground. In this manner, the runner will slide into the ball and not under it.

Plays in the infield

Infield plays usually involve a difficult chance. For instance, on a bunt or a topped ground ball, the catcher must quickly jump from behind the plate and catch up to the ball (Figure 6.6). Then he must quickly decide where to throw. In

Figure 6.6   Catcher must quickly get out of box on topped ground ball.

some cases it might take a bare-handed scoop, which is not the easiest play to make.

Fielding the bunt involves two difficult problems for the catcher. First of all, he must get out from behind the plate quickly without interfering with the hitter. Usually he has little chance of interfering with a left-handed batter. The right-hander presents another problem. If the right-handed hitter gets a slow start, then the catcher could beat him out of the box. On the other hand, if the right-hander gets a good start, the catcher must wait until the bunter has passed him before going out to make the play.

Another problem on a bunt is to throw to the second baseman covering first and not hit the runner with the throw. Actually, a runner should be called out if he runs inside of the base line. But this is a difficult call for the umpire to make and he often fails to notice the violation.

A good, smart catcher will always alert the umpire to a possible play at first. Then the umpire will watch for the possible interference play. In any case, this is a tough play for the catcher to make, and it should be practiced many times by the young catcher. One of the best ways to do this is to use an actual runner so that you will get used to making the throws just as you would in an actual ball game.

A catcher also has a difficult play on a dropped third strike. On a play of this type you can sometimes move to the inside of the diamond to get a better angle for making the throw. In the event you can't, it may be necessary to make the peg to the foul line side of first base. Once again, the best way to work on this play is to use a runner in practice, just as it would happen in an actual game.

Throwing to second base on a bunt or a topped grounder is a little easier than making the throw to first base. On this play it's important for the catcher to know ahead of time who is going to cover second base. Since the throw may have to be made while the shortstop or second baseman is running toward the bag, it is doubly important for the catcher to know who is covering.

Catching the base thief

In fast pitch the base runner may not leave the base until the ball leaves the pitcher's hands. With a right-hander at bat, the catcher is able to watch the runner out of the corner of his eye and will see the base runner leaving the base. With a left-hander at bat this is more difficult and the catcher must be more alert. When he sees the base runner preparing to make a break, he must first catch the ball cleanly and with the proper glove placement. A ball that comes in high should be caught with the finger portion of the glove pointing up (Figure 6.7), while the finger portion should be pointed down on low pitches (Figure 6.8).

Once the catch is made cleanly, the catcher quickly gets the ball out of his glove, cocks his arm, and steps forward with his left foot.

The throw should go slightly to the right of the bag, one to two feet above the ground. If the peg goes to the left side

Figure 6.7   Position of mitt on high
pitches.

Figure 6.8   Position of mitt on low
pitches.

of the bag, the fielder has to make a backhand stab and still
try to make a tag on the sliding runner.

Throwing consistently and accurately to second base
comes through practice, something the young catcher should
do often. The first step is to adjust to the distance from home
to second base, which is 85 feet. A young catcher can work
alone throwing at an open barrel or a target placed on a box.

After getting used to the regulation distance, it's better
to practice under actual game conditions. Receiving a
pitched ball and then throwing to the fielder moving to cover
second base is the best way to do this. If at all possible, a base
runner should also be used.

Slow pitch

A slow-pitch catcher has less responsibility than a fast-
pitch catcher. Slow-pitch rules do not permit bunting or
stealing. So the catcher's main job is to protect home plate.

Because there are many more runs scored in slow pitch, the job of protecting home plate is indeed an important one.

As in fast pitch, the catcher assumes the role of team leader. He or she should be a "holler" person and keep teammates aware of the count and how many outs there are at all times. Another job is remembering where each batter is likely to hit the ball. Since the catcher is in the perfect spot to see all fielders, he should adjust teammates' positions when the batter is coming up to the plate.

Because a slow-pitch catcher does not have to contend with bunting or stealing, there's no need for a really strong arm. Catching is one position in slow pitch for the big, slow person who can hit the ball a country mile.

Photograph by R. Schreul

7

Hitting and running

The rookie hitter

A beginning softball hitter should not settle on a bat just because it's a model used by a famous ball player. He must feel comfortable with the bat he chooses. Although a heavy bat will normally give a little more distance, there's no advantage if the young hitter can't bring it around in time. Length is another point to consider in selecting a bat. Any bat that is too long will cause as many problems as a bat that's too heavy. In most instances, the length of the bat is stamped on the end of the handle.

A young hitter should "choke up" on the bat. Choking up means that he moves his hands up a few inches towards the large end of the bat (Figure 7.1). This will give him much better control. Some of the finest hitters in fast pitch choke up on every pitch. The majority of softball players prefer the medium grip (Figure 7.2). Many players take a long grip (Figure 7.3) on the first two strikes and then shorten the grip on the last strike.

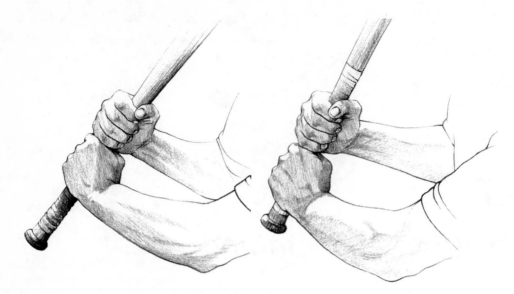

Figure 7.1 The choke grip is recommended for beginners. Good "punch" hitters often use this type of grip.

Figure 7.2 Medium grip is used by the majority of softball players.

Figure 7.3 Long-ball hitters usually use the long grip.

Finding a comfortable stance is one of the most important steps in learning to hit. The three basic stances used are: (1) the open stance, (2) the closed stance, and (3) the square stance.

In the open stance (Figure 7.4) the front foot is placed farther from the plate than the rear foot. This type of stance is usually used by the pull hitter. In the closed stance (Figure 7.5) the front foot is placed closer to the plate. An opposite field hitter often uses this stance. In the square stance (Figure 7.6) both feet are the same distance from the plate. Most hitters prefer the square stance. In this stance the feet are pointing directly toward the plate, with the legs spread about 12 to 18 inches apart.

There are several points that are key to every batting stance, no matter where the feet are placed. When the hitter is set for the pitch, he takes an almost erect position. Knees are slightly bent with the weight evenly distributed on the balls of the feet. Hips and shoulders are level, and the arms, with elbows bent, are held away from the body.

Most batters hold the bat at about the same angle. In fast pitch, it is best for the elbow of the rear arm to be held shoulder high. In this position, the hitter can get up on the

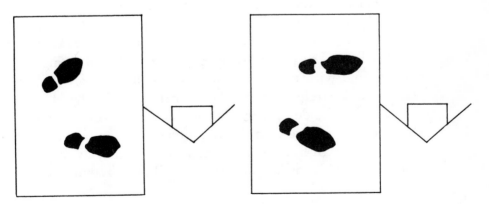

Figure 7.4   Open stance.   Figure 7.5   Closed stance.

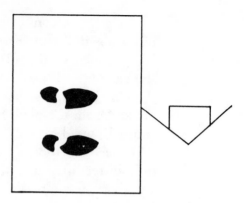

Figure 7.6   Square stance.

rise ball more easily. If the hitter consistently drops the rear elbow, he frequently has trouble hitting the rise ball.

Get set

There should be total concentration by the hitter as he prepares for the pitch. A good hitter dismisses everything from his mind as he approaches the plate. Getting ready to hit (Figure 7.7) is just as important as any other part of hitting. Regardless of what's going on in the field or in the stands, the hitter should be concentrating only on the pitcher. It's a personal contest between pitcher and hitter.

Watching the pitcher before you get into the batter's box is a big advantage. While you're in the dugout, keep an eye on his every move. Many hitters get set and swing the bat in time with the pitch's delivery as they are waiting on the on-deck circle. Observe the pitcher to see if he prefers to pitch fast. If he does, then slow him down in the batter's box by stepping out occasionally. If a pitcher likes to take a lot of time, always rush up to the batting box as quickly as possible. In other words, always try to break his rhythm.

At the plate

Get the bat in a ready position once your stance feels

Figure 7.7   Ready position: Weight
is evenly distributed on balls of
feet. Hips and shoulders are level,
with arms held away from body.

comfortable. Some hitters prefer to swing the bat several times before the pitcher throws the first pitch. If you're comfortable doing this, fine. But, in most cases, extra swinging only takes energy and wastes time.

Many coaches and instructional manuals tell the hitter to maintain a level swing. This needs further explanation. Of course, if the ball comes right down the middle of the plate, belt high; the swing will be level. However, there is no way you can hit a drop ball knee-high with a level swing. In hitting a drop, use a swing similar to the one you use in hitting a golf ball. On the other hand, to hit a rise ball, you have to get above or on top of it. It can almost be a downward swing. A coach must explain that swinging level means "keeping the bat in a true arc." Dropping or lobbing the bat will hurt the hitter's swing.

Remember to keep from swinging too hard. Of course, everyone wants to hit with power. The harder the swing, the farther the ball goes. But beginners who continually swing

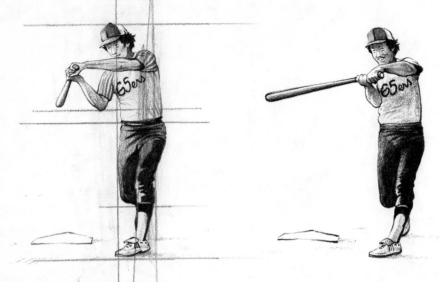

Figure 7.8   As pitch is delivered, stride begins with wrists cocked. Weight is transferred to front foot.

Figure 7.9   At point of contact, front leg is straight with rear leg bent slightly.

hard often develop an underswing. An underswing makes it difficult for the batter to hit a rise ball. In most cases, overswinging goes along with a long stride, which is also harmful for hitting the rise ball.

For fast pitch, a short stride of about six to eight inches is usually best. However, in slow pitch this is not necessarily true. A longer stride will usually not affect the slow-pitch hitter that much.

The foot is slid forward just slightly above the ground. The forward stride should be timed with the pitcher's delivery. If the hitter strides too early or too late, it affects timing. An overanxious hitter normally hurries the stride. He or she will swing ahead of the ball, or miss it in trying to adjust timing. Hitters who always stride early can sometimes delay the stride by twisting the front hip toward the plate just prior to the stride. A slight twist will delay the stride just enough to get the arms into proper hitting position.

Figure 7.10 Cocked wrists and bent arms end up with arms fully extended on follow-through.

Above all, keep the stride straight ahead. Beginners should work hard on this phase of hitting. Once the beginner gets into the habit of stepping away from the plate, he will have many problems trying to change the habit later on.

With the pitch

As the pitch leaves the pitcher's hand, the stride begins and the wrists are cocked (Figure 7.8). A hitter has a much better chance to hit a variety of pitches with the wrists cocked. Arms are fully extended at the end of the swing. Full power of the swing will be achieved at the time of contact. At this point, the weight that was formerly on the rear foot is transferred to the front foot. The front leg is kept straight while the rear leg is bent when contact is made (Figure 7.9).

If a hitter has trouble popping up, he should check for a bent front leg or a long stride. This may not be the only reason, but it's one fault that can be easily rectified. At the end of the swing, the wrists roll over and the follow-through is completed (Figure 7.10). If every part of the swing is right, the follow-through will take care of itself.

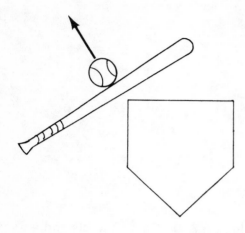

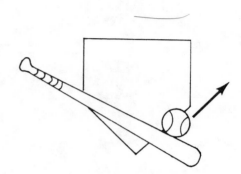

Figure 7.11   It's best to meet the inside pitch in front of the plate.

Figure 7.12   Hitters should not try to pull outside pitch. Outside pitch is met at rear of plate.

Hit where it's pitched

Whether you're playing baseball, fast pitch, or slow pitch, hit the ball where it's pitched. This means that if the ball is pitched inside, it should be met in front of the plate (Figure 7.11) and pulled to left field. It would be pulled to right field if you're left-handed.

When it's pitched across the heart, or center, of the plate, the ball is hit straight across the plate and is driven to center field (Figure 7.13). When the ball is pitched to the outside of the plate, contact should be made at the rear of the plate (Figure 7.12). A right-handed hitter should hit the outside pitch to right field, and the left-handed hitter hits the outside pitch to left field.

Sometimes it's not easy to hit the ball where it's pitched, especially when you're facing a top-notch pitcher. When a hitter persistently tries to pull an outside pitch, more than likely he will never get a solid hit. When you try to pull an outside pitch, there's a good chance you'll miss the ball completely or meet it on the end of the bat. This usually results in weakly hit ground balls or pop flies. A hitter who

Drag bunt

When the drag bunt is executed properly, it should surprise the defensive infielders. A hitter begins his normal stride and swing, but at the last moment he slides his top hand up the bat. Actually, the top hand is moved while the ball is on its way. A good drag bunter moves the top hand up about six to eight inches rather than up to the trademark as in the sacrifice bunt. Proper execution of the drag bunt allows a hitter to get a big jump toward first base. As the batter takes his normal stride, he makes contact with the ball as the front foot is planted. This is one continuous motion as the batter breaks for first. The hitter is really bunting and running at the same time (Figure 7.15).

Base running

Although natural speed is a big help, getting a quick start is the most important part of good base running. There are many exceptionally speedy runners who do not run the

Figure 7.15 The hitter is actually running and bunting at the same time on the drag bunt.

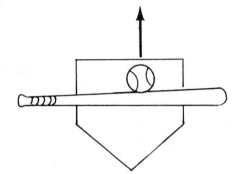

Figure 7.13 Ball pitched over heart of plate is hit into middle of the diamond.

fails to meet the inside pitch in front of the plate usually hits it on the handle.

Raising the batting average

Whether or not you have natural ability, there are certain fundamentals regarding hitting that must be considered. If you want to maintain a good batting average against good pitching, you have to face good pitching often. A hitter who has trouble hitting a rise ball has a much better chance of improving by facing a good rise-ball pitcher frequently.

Hitting is like fielding or any other part of the game. You must do it often to do it well. Even if you receive good instructions from a fine hitter on all aspects of hitting, practice and more practice is still the answer to better hitting. Besides regular practice, you should have a steady progression in the type of competition you face. Young hitters may face average pitching for one, two, or several seasons in a row. When they face an outstanding pitcher, they're obviously going to have problems. At this time, the difficulty in hitting has nothing to do with basic techniques. It's due to the fact that they are beginners and are not used to hitting against a good pitcher. A coach or manager should be careful not to make any drastic changes at this time in the basic stance or swing. Once the youngsters face better pitchers, they often start meeting the ball more consistently.

The bunt

There are two types of bunts used in fast pitch: the sacrifice bunt and the bunt for a hit, also called a drag bunt. If a bunt is well placed, it can be just as important as an extra-base hit. However, a beginner should spend time learning to put the bunt down properly rather than trying to place it in any particular spot. On a sacrifice bunt, the aim of the bunter is to move the runner to the next base. You should not worry about getting out of the box fast. Your main concern in this situation is to get the ball down fair without popping it up.

When a hitter sacrifices, he or she stands in front of the batter's box since this provides a better chance to get the bunt down fair. When the pitcher begins the delivery, you bring your rear foot forward and even with the front one. Normally, feet are spread approximately 12 to 18 inches. Some hitters feel more comfortable standing very close to the plate. In this case, the front foot is moved backward and placed even with the rear foot. Whichever style is used on a sacrifice bunt, you should be facing the pitcher with hands well spread on the bat (Figure 7.14).

The position of the bat should be parallel to the ground with the lower hand in the normal spot near the handle. The other hand should be resting near the trademark. As you move into the bunting stance, never move the bottom hand. Slide the top hand up to a spot near the trademark. Knees and hips should be slightly bent, with the weight on the balls of your feet. The top hand is actually used to steady the bat. Most players let the bat rest loosely on the tips of the fingers. The thumb grips the top part of the bat.

When the ball approaches, the bat is held still, almost as if the hitter were going to catch the ball on the bat. When

Figure 7.14 On sacrifice bunt hitter squares around pitcher.

bunted properly, the pitch should make contact o part of the bat. This way, the ball heads toward On the other hand, when the ball hits the top o will be popped up, creating a possible double pla

In most instances, the best direction to bunt the pitcher, since the first and third basemen tight on the sacrifice bunt. When bunting towar the bat is placed straight across the plate. Ac ment of the bunt is difficult in fast pitch, but by adjusting the bat properly. For example, hitter wishing to bunt toward third base, plac angle similar to that of a pull hitter as he m front of the plate. On a bunt to first, the ang quite similar to an opposite field hitter m swing in that direction.

bases well. For example, a wide turn can cost the runner valuable seconds, no matter how fast he is.

A good third-base or first-base coach can be a big asset to the base runner. When a ball is hit to right or right center field, a hitter can see where the ball is going. He can judge himself whether or not to take an extra base.

When the ball is hit to left field, however, a runner must look for a signal from the first-base coach. Trying to look where the ball went costs the runner extra time. In some cases, he may even miss first base.

Once the hitter knows he has hit a fair ball into the outfield, he should run about two to three feet outside the first-base foul line. Approaching the bag, he adjusts his stride to make a sharp turn and touch the inside corner of the bag with the right foot. On a single, he rounds the bag, stops, and quickly checks to see if the fielder has possession of the ball. A good runner is always alert in case the outfielder bobbles the ball or makes a poor throw to the lead base. Never turn your back on the play.

On a possible extra-base hit, a runner heading for second must make a quick decision about what to do, deciding whether to slide, stand up, or round the base. If the runner rounds second base, and particularly on hits to righ field, he should look for the third-base coach for help. A runner usually can make up his own mind on an extra-base hit to left or center field. As a runner approaches either second or third, he should run slightly to the outfield side of the base path. This way he can make a sharp turn as he touches the inside of the bag with his right foot.

Stealing

A good base stealer not only gets a quick start, he learns to anticipate the pitcher's release of the ball. Anticipating the release is probably more important than speed, since the runner cannot leave the base until the ball leaves the

Figure 7.16　Correct approach on　　Figure 7.17　Correct approach on
　　　　　　　hook slide.　　　　　　　　　　　　straight-in slide.

pitcher's hand. No matter how speedy a runner is, if he waits until the ball leaves the pitcher's hand and then breaks, he is not likely to steal many bases. On the break from the base, the base stealer should be on the move at the exact moment the ball leaves the pitcher's hand.

Sliding

There are two advantages in making a proper slide: (1) it gives the runner another chance of being safe on the tag play, and (2) it prevents injuries. There are three basic types of slides. The first is the hook slide (Figure 7.16), also called the fallaway. Another is the straight-in slide (Figure 7.17), and the third is the head-first slide. The head-first slide is not recommended for the beginner.

Figure 7.18   Proper position for completion of hook slide.

A straight-in slide is executed by keeping the top leg straight while the bottom leg is bent sharply at the knee. When the runner hits the bag with the front foot, the bottom leg is drawn up. This allows the runner to gain his footing very quickly.

The hook slide is used to avoid an infielder's tag. It's executed by first hurling the body away from the infielder and then hooking the bag with the right toe when sliding to the left of the base. This procedure is reversed if the slide is made to the right of the bag (Figure 7.18).

Hitting—slow pitch

Although the ball drops down to the hitter in slow pitch, stance, stride, wrist action, and swing must be well coordinated, as described in the fast-pitch section of this chapter. It takes a little while to adjust your timing in slow pitch if you have previously played baseball or fast-pitch softball.

Swinging too hard is a common mistake made by newcomers to slow pitch. A good smooth swing with fast waist action will accomplish just as much as the lunging and choppy action that usually accompanies the hard swing.

When the pitch passes over the plate at armpit height, the hitter must get up on top of the ball keeping the elbow of his rear arm from dipping down too low. On a knee-high pitch, a golf-type swing with good wrist action is required.

Hitting the ball where it's pitched applies just as much, or even more so, in slow pitch than it does in fast pitch. A good place hitter who hits the ball where it's pitched can maintain a very high batting average.

Slow pitch is an ideal sport for a big, powerful, long-ball hitter who is a reasonably good fielder. Positions such as catcher, third base, and first base do not require players with good running speed. That's why the long-ball hitter with average speed can play slow pitch for many, many seasons.

Glossary

Assist—A play in which two or more players handle the ball to complete the putout.

Back up—a position taken by one fielder behind another in case the ball gets past the first fielder.

Bad hop—an unusual or tricky bounce of a batted or thrown ball.

Bag—another term for base.

"Ball"—a pitch not struck at by the batter that fails to fall in the strike zone (see rules for strike zone).

Baseline—the marked or imaginary line between the bases.

Batter's box—the area to which the batter is restricted while in position to hit a pitched ball.

Batting practice—the period of time allowed for players to practice hitting before a game.

Batting slump—the period of time when a hitter's batting average drops below his or her normal average.

Batting stance—the position taken by a batter awaiting a pitched ball.

Blocking the plate—taking the tag in crouch position, usually a move by the catcher, to keep a runner from scoring a run at home plate. Glove hand is in front of the plate and on the ground.

Breaking pitch—the movement of a pitched ball from a straight line; that is, the break of a curve.

Chance—another term for making a play.

Change-up—a slowed pitch sent by a pitcher at his or her normal pitching speed.

Clean catch—a catch made by a fielder without bobbling or juggling the ball.

Chopper—a high-bouncing batted ball.

Chucker—the pitcher.

Closed stance—a type of stance, with front foot closer to the plate, taken by the hitter as he waits for the pitch (see Chapter 7, "Hitting and running").

Covering a base—moving to a base to take the throw for a putout.

Curve—a pitched ball that moves in a curving line rather than a straight line.

Cut-off man—a player, usually an infielder, who intentionally intercepts a throw instead of allowing the ball to go where it was originally intended.

Double—a two-base hit.

Double play—a play by the defensive team in which two offensive players are legally put out in one continuous play.

Double steal—a play in which two offensive players each steal a base on a continuous play.

Dropped third strike—a failure by the catcher to hold on to the ball on a third strike. Batter can run and try to reach first on this play.

Error—a mistake by a defensive player.

Extra-base hit—a base hit where the hitter gets more than one base.

First sacker—the first baseman.

Fly ball—a batted ball hit into the air.

Follow-through—the act of continuing a motion in throwing or hitting.

Force-out—an out that can be made only when a base runner loses the right to the base he is occupying because the batter becomes a baserunner and before the batter or a succeeding baserunner has been put out. (No tag is needed.)

Foul line—the lines that enclose the field from home plate to the outfield.

Foul tip—a batted ball that goes directly from the bat, not higher than the batter's head, into the catcher's hands.

Glove—equipment used by infielders as an aid in catching the ball. A glove has five finger placements.

Ground ball—a batted ball that rolls along the ground.

Grounder—a ground ball.

Hit and run—an offensive play in which the baserunner leaves with the pitch. The second baseman moves to cover second, and the hitter then tries to hit the ball through the hole left by the second baseman.

Hit away—a situation in which the batter is swinging for a hit and not bunting.

Home run—a base hit that enables the batter either to hit the ball fairly over the outfield fence or circle the bases on a hit that doesn't go over the fence.

Hook slide—a sliding action performed by the baserunner to avoid a tag. The bag is hooked with the toe.

Infielder—the first baseman, second baseman, third baseman, or shortstop. Pitchers and catchers are also considered infielders.

In-shoot—a type of pitch that breaks in toward the batter, sometimes referred to as a screwball.

Inside pitch—a pitched ball that either fails to pass over the plate or barely passes over the batter's side of the plate.

Keystone sack—second base.

Let-up—a change-up or slow ball.

Line drive—a batted ball that stays on a straight line instead of going high into the air or onto the ground.

Mask—safety equipment that straps around the catcher's head and serves as a protective covering for the face.

Mitt—playing equipment similar to a glove, except that the thumb portion is separated from the other part of the mitt. Only the first baseman and the catcher may wear a mitt.

On-deck circle—a marked circle in foul territory where the next batter in the lineup awaits his turn to hit.

On-deck hitter—the next batter in the lineup waiting to bat.

Open stance—a type of stance a batter assumes with the front foot farther from the plate than the rear foot as he awaits the pitch (see Chapter 7, "Hitting and running").

Opposite field hitter—a batter who usually hits the ball to the opposite field from where it's expected; that is, most right-handed hitters hit the ball to left field and most left-handed hitters hit the ball to right field.

Outfielder—a player who normally plays an outfield position—left, right, or center field.

Outside pitch—a pitched ball that either fails to pass over that portion of the plate farthest from the batter or just barely passes over it.

Pick-off play—a defensive play usually started by the catcher to catch a runner off base.

Pinch hitter—a batter who is substituted for another batter already in the game.

Pitching rubber—the wood or rubber rectangle on which the pitcher stands to pitch the ball.

Pivot foot—the foot on which body weight is shifted. Also, the foot a pitcher must keep in contact with the pitcher's plate until the ball is released.

Play deep—plays farther back—the position taken by either an infielder or outfielder in backing up from normal position.

Pop-up—a batted ball hit high in the air and almost directly above the infield or shallow outfield.

Presentation—a holding or stopped position the pitcher takes just before beginning his or her windup.

Pull hitter—a batter who consistently hits to one side of the field; that is, a right-handed hitter who always hits to left field or a left-handed hitter who consistently hits to right field.

Putout—a play other than a strike-out in which the hitter or baserunner is called out.

Quick hands—the ability to field and throw the ball quickly and efficiently.

Relay man—a fielder, usually an infielder, who takes a throw from an outfielder and throws it on to another infielder.

Relay throw—the throw made to the relay man or the throw made by the relay man.

Rise ball—a pitched ball that deviates from a straight line, moving upward.

Rundown—a defensive play in which one or more players attempt to tag a baserunner who is trapped between bases.

Sacrifice bunt—an offensive play in which the batter taps (bunts) a pitched ball fairly to advance a runner even though he will most likely be put out himself.

Screwball—a pitched ball that moves in toward a batter, also called an in-shoot.

Second sacker—the second baseman.

Shin guards—protective devices, which are strapped to the front of the catcher's lower legs and knees.

Shortstop—the player who plays between second and third base.

Sign—a visible movement of the hand, arm, or leg (a code) by a coach. This code tells the hitter and the runner or both what to do on a certain pitch.

Signal—a visible code from catcher to pitcher that tells the pitcher what pitch to throw. It is usually given with the fingers of the throwing hand.

Single—a base hit by a batter that advances him or her to first base.

Slingshot—a style of delivery used by pitchers in fast pitch.

Spikes—metal, rubber, or plastic cleats attached to a player's shoes to give better footing.

Squares around—settles into position. The position a batter takes in preparing to place a sacrifice bunt.

Square stance—a position taken by a batter as he prepares to hit; both feet are the same distance from the plate.

Squeeze play—an offensive move used when a runner is on third base. As the ball is pitched, the runner immediately runs for home plate and the hitter bunts the ball (fast pitch only).

Steal—an offensive move in which the runner leaves with the pitch and attempts to advance without being thrown out by the catcher (fast pitch only).

Steals signal—a strategy move whereby one team learns the other team's code. For example, a baserunner could detect the catcher's signals to the pitcher.

Steps in bucket—an incorrect stride by a batter in which he steps away from the pitch rather than striding straight ahead.

Straight-in slide—a move by a runner to avoid a tag by sliding straight into the base.

Stretching a hit—an attempt by a hitter to try for an additional base.

Strike zone (fast pitch)—the zone in which a pitched ball passes over any part of home plate between the batter's armpits and the top of his knees when the batter assumes his natural batting stance.

Strike zone (slow pitch)—the zone in which a pitched ball passes over any part of home plate between the batter's highest shoulder and his knees when the batter assumes his natural batting stance.

Stuff—the movement or break of the pitched ball; that is, curve, drop, rise ball, in-shoot, change-up, etc.

Tag (out)—a putout completed by a fielder touching the runner with the ball.

Third sacker—the third baseman.

Topped ball—a batted ball hit at the top by the batter, which causes it to bounce on the ground.

Triple—a three-base hit.

Walk—the awarding of first base by the umpire after he has called four "balls."

Warm-up—the time used in exercise by a pitcher or other players in preparing to play.

Windmill—a type of pitching style in fast pitch (see Chapter 5, "The pitcher").

Wind sprint—fast running for a short distance by a player in warming up.

Windup—a movement of the pitcher's arms and body in preparation for delivering the ball to a batter.

Index

Index